What people are saying about *Charlotte Ann* and *Pre...*

I'm sick of the glut of phony "purpose" books on the Christian market today. Most are just clever attempts to capitalize on what some have turned into a religious buzzword. Charlotte Ann's is different and embedded with a reality with God, truly resplendent with God's purpose, not ours. Life is unpredictable, but God promises to bring us to an expected end. As Charlotte Ann shows in a masterful rendering, He uses both the failed and exultant experiences of our lives to persevere—and manifest—his purpose.

DL FOSTER
Author, *Touching a Dead Man*

I LOVE your soulful book! Let's hear it for the people like you who have been there, done that, and have come out of it all as a WINNER! You are blessed, and therefore your readers will be blessed. Hurry and get this book published for all to read.

PETEY PARKER
Author, *Corporate Kitty Litter*, *Body Language and Soulful Thoughts* and *Blueprint for Success* (co-authored with Stephen Covey and Ken Blanchard)

The sample chapter is awesome! It is transparent like an onion being peeled layer upon layer; and just as an onion produces tears, so do our war wounds, which in turn produce scars. The author, Charlotte Ann Moore, does an awesome job conveying the message that we did not just happen on this earth for no good reason; like the title of her book, we were "preserved for a purpose." I can't wait to read the rest!

NANCI DES GERLAIS
Author, *Muddy Waters: An Insider's View of Native Spirituality*

The chapter excerpts I read from your book were very readable. It was an easy read that captured my interest because of its relevance. I know that anyone who purchases this book will be inspired to continue the course God has designed for them with assurance and passion. Keep going forward and following God's plan for your life.

ALGERITA EVANS-ANDY
Educator

Insightful and enlightening.

LORI DEE MOORE

MORE What People Are Saying

Awesome! Awesome! I've never had the pleasure of meeting you, but after reading the sneak peek, I felt like I had. As a pastor, I am much aware of the many issues and challenges that the Christian believer is dealing with on a daily basis but feel that to reveal such is an indictment against their faith and love for God. It's high time that we produce books that deal with real struggles of personal development and relationships from the basis of spiritual principles with the goal of building a bridge between the two. I truly enjoyed what I read thus far and look forward to the finished product. It will be a must read for the saint who's tired of faking that all is well and ready to learn how to take the appropriate steps to truly make it all well! Continue to walk in the blessing!

STAN FERRELL
Pastor, Treasures of Excellence Ministries, Arlington, TX

It is so wonderful to see that you are fulfilling one of your long awaited dreams. To publish a book! I remember meeting with you and how you shared some of your dreams years ago. So glad you stepped out on your own "by faith" to fulfill your purpose. You are an excellent writer. . . . I love the title you have chosen.

Blessings & favor to you and your ministry!

SHERRY FERRIS
Associate Pastor, The Heartland Church, Irving, TX

Expecting the complete work with high expectations of the whole being as good as the excerpts. God can be felt in your writing.

BISHOP JACKIE GOODEN
Pastor, St. Paul Baptist Church, Marshall, TX

You are amazing and wonderful.

BISHOP CASEY MINER
FaithBeto Ministry, Huntsville, TX

Preserved for a Purpose

Make your Move from Surviving to Thriving

Charlotte Ann
Moore

Charmedia Publishing
A division of Charmedia, Inc.

www.CharmediaPublishing.com

Published by Charmedia Publishing
www.CharmediaPublishing.com

Copyright © 2011 Charlotte Ann Moore

All rights reserved. No portion of this book may be reproduced, sorted in a retrieval system, or transmitted in any form or by any means—electronic, mechanical, photocopy, recording, scanning, or other—except for brief, in context quotations in critical reviews or articles, without the prior written permission of the publisher.

All trademarks and copyrighted items mentioned in this publication are the trademarks or copyrights of their respective registrants.

Editor: Melanie Mallon

Editorial assistance: Brenda Quinn, Roger Boykin, Martee Lew
Cover design: Elohim, Charlotte Ann Moore, Keith Fink/The Master's Press
Chapter illustrations by Keith Fink/The Master's Press

Interior design: Keith Fink/The Master's Press
Cover photography: Sam Martinez
Author Photo: Liz Marquez/LM Photography
Charmedia, Inc. logo: Steve Deitz/SD Creative
Printing by The Master's Press/Dallas, TX

Published in Dallas, Texas, by Charmedia Publishing, a division of Charmedia, Inc.

Scripture quotations marked KJV are from The Holy Bible, KING JAMES VERSION.

Scripture quotations marked NIV are taken from The Holy Bible, NEW INTERNATIONAL VERSION.
Copyright © 1973, 1978, 1984 by International Bible Society.
Used by permission of Zondervan Bible Publishing House. All rights reserved.

The "NIV" and "New International Version" trademarks are registered in the
United States Patent and Trademark Office by International Bible Society.
Use of other trademark requires the permission of International Bible Society.

Scripture taken from The Message. Copyright © 1993, 1994, 1995, 1996, 2000, 2001, 2002.
Used by permission of NavPress Publishing Group.

Library of Congress Cataloging-in-Publication Data

Moore, Charlotte Ann.

Preserved for a Purpose—Make Your Move from Surviving to Thriving / Charlotte Ann Moore.

p.cm.
Includes bibliographical references.
ISBN 978- 0-9797434-0-5 (paperback)

    Self-help. 2. Religious life - Christianity. 3. Success—Psychological aspects. 4. Self-actualization.
    1. Title: Preserved for a Purpose II. Make Your Move from Surviving to Thriving.

    Printed in the United States of America.

Charmedia Publishing books and other materials are available at special discounts for bulk purchases in the U.S. by corporations, institutions, and other organizations. For more information, please contact the Special Markets Department at Charmedia Publishing by e-mailing Info@CharmediaPublishing.com.

Dedication

To my parents, I.D. and Daisy Moore

Purpose is forever.

Table of Contents

Introduction		1

Part One — **How Did We Get Here?**

Chapter 1	Meltdown Moments	7
Chapter 2	Shadow Seasons	25
Chapter 3	Site Planning	49

Part Two — **Go Get Your Life Back**

Chapter 4	Laying Your Foundation	67
Chapter 5	Building Your House	83
Chapter 6	Furnishing and Decorating	93
Chapter 7	Scar Stories and Star Stories	109
Chapter 8	Finish Well	123

Introduction

There are people in this world who reach midlife having done everything right. They planned their lives out at puberty. They attended the right schools, married the perfect spouses on the first (or second) try, and raised beautiful children who grew into relatively well-adjusted adults. They never got in too far over their heads in debt. They chose the right career paths from the beginning, made transitions as necessary, and stayed in those careers nearly their entire lives.

And now, these perfect people look forward to or are experiencing relatively comfortable retirements (or second careers) because they saved enough, invested carefully, and made adjustments when needed.

I didn't write this book for them.

Then there are the *nearly* perfect people—people who have done *almost* everything right. Sure, they've experienced hardships and setbacks: a layoff here, a divorce or breakup there, raising difficult kids, caring for aging parents, "market corrections." But they've managed to shine on with a sunny attitude and a quick comeback.

I didn't write this book for them either.

I wrote this book for the rest of us—the real, highly *im*perfect people who live real, imperfect lives—we survivors who've walked through Death Valley and brought back lizards as a souvenir.

I'm one of those imperfect people. I've been where you are, and in many ways I'm still there. I understand you because I *am* you. Every day I live what I'm talking about. My passion is to help *us* become our best, no matter where we start from.

Perhaps I wrote this book for myself.

I wrote *Preserved for a Purpose* for people who have given up on life—and for people who feel that life has given up on them. We've been hampered by problems, poverty, and our pasts. We've been shipwrecked time and time again. People like us have been hamstrung by procrastination, fear, anger, bitterness, and self-doubt. We're the people who have survived broken promises, broken hearts, broken relationships, and broken dreams. Even broken spirits.

And yet . . . *we're still here*. We've managed to make lives for ourselves despite extreme adversity. We keep coming back—sometimes wondering why—even though we've been counted out over and over again.

I wrote this book to speak a word of life and success to those who have grown far too accustomed to living to less than their potential. We've made lives for ourselves, all the while wondering whether life offers *more*.

In *Preserved for a Purpose*, you'll find principles for making the rest of your days count. Here, we'll extract the purpose from the pain, the promise from the pitfalls, and your dreams from your defeats. You'll learn how to put together the life tools you need to get ready for your Big Dreams. You'll better discern who should be around you on the journey, who shouldn't—and why. Here, we'll walk together in our lifelong journey to our purpose and destiny.

Another thing as we begin: I am unapologetically, unashamedly a Christian. My writing reflects my faith that not only is Jesus Christ, as He Himself said, *the* Way to eternal life, but that His Word is Truth and provides illumination to achieve the divine purpose planted in us before we were born. As His principles were planted in me, I pass them on to you. I'm writing to each of you in faith that no matter what your beliefs are or where your spiritual life is right now, by the time you finish reading, you will be healed, encouraged, and empowered by what flows from the heart of God through me to you.

Know that I am praying for each one of you. May you be informed, inspired, motivated, and blessed.

Part One

How Did I Get Here?

I don't mind dying—I just want to *live* before I do it.

Charlotte Ann Moore

CHAPTER ONE — MELTDOWN MOMENTS

Meltdown Moments

Chapter 1

"How did I get here?!" I stood in my cramped bathroom, screaming and moaning. It was 3 a.m. I stared sleeplessly into the mirror under the harsh makeup lights. My face was on fire from the dental cavity that had unleashed its fury on my unsuspecting mouth. No oral gel, no clove oil, no positive thought to free my mind from the pain could comfort me.

Normally, I pride myself on not being a "weepy woman." But the pain had drained away my pride hours ago. I desperately willed myself to pull it together while uncontrollable sobs wrecked my usually sunny demeanor. Without warning, in the midst of my physical pain, waves of mental anguish began to flood my soul. Out of nowhere, apropos of nothing, every failure I'd experienced and every fear I'd dreaded began to play itself on the silver screen of my mind: Broken relationships, painful abandonments, ridiculously bad choices danced mockingly before me. Incomplete projects, lost jobs, business deals gone badly. Life-altering decisions. Financial tsunamis. Spiritual and emotional abuse. Ministry rejection. Personal rejection. Chronic illness that caused my weight to creep up to an all-time high. It was the scariest of scary movies; all my life's disappointments marched on my unwilling memory like an unrelenting army. I was powerless to stop the continuous loop of suffering.

My mind, will, and emotions were under attack. A horde of demonic forces marshaled itself against me, each voice urging me to give up: *No one wants to hear what you have to say. . . you're a joke. No one cares about you, your writing, OR your ministry. No one truly "gets it" about you. No one wants to be your true friend. No man wants you for his wife. Your health is a wreck. Your life is a waste. Why . . . don't . . . you . . . just . . . give . . . up?*

Not just give up my writing. Not just give up my ministries. Not just give up my dreams. Give up . . . *my life.*

I was in a battle for my destiny that cold October Saturday.

Later that morning, I drove across town to an available dentist. While I waited my turn, I curled myself in a fetal position on the frigid floor of his '70s-furnished bathroom. Eventually, the dentist eased my physical pain by performing a root canal. But by then, the emotional boil had come to a head. I was in the middle of a Meltdown Moment.

How did I get here? If I had written my life's script, it surely wouldn't have ended up like this. I'd had a successful beginning; I had two loving, married, parents, who had welcomed my arrival. I started reading spontaneously at 18 months old. My core skill was established from the time I was 14. I'd earned two bachelor's degrees from a prestigious university. I'd been able to travel and see a bit of the world. Surely by now I would have published a half-dozen best-sellers and launched several successful media ventures. I would have had the house, the husband, the 2.4 kids, and the dog by now. (I already had the cat.) My ministry work should have blessed people around the world. Instead, I was having a Meltdown Moment on a dental office bathroom floor.

How Did We Get Here?

Meltdown Moments happen when your dreams collide head-on with your reality. We all were born with ideas, gifts, and talents that are designed to lead us into our purpose and destiny, Big Dreams I call them, implanted within us. Some of them have barely germinated. Some of them are in seedling stage. Some of them are in danger of being choked out by weeds, our life experiences, and Meltdown Moments. See, like the fertilizer of faith nurtures your dreams, Meltdown Moments can mortally damage them. What others say about you won't necessarily affect you, but what *you* think about you definitely will. We'll discuss Big Dreams in detail a bit later in Chapter 3.

Most of us have had Meltdown Moments, whether private or public. I know I'm not the only one. Have you ever looked back at parts of your life and wondered, *What happened?* Your Meltdown Moments may not have been as dramatic as mine. Some appear quietly: You seem collected and together on the outside. The way you act, look, live, work, socialize, dress, spend, and drive speaks success. Your external affairs are in order. Your finances are on point. You look like you have it all together; you've trained yourself not to let anyone see you sweat. In reality, you're one pluck away from your last nerve. Whether your Meltdown Moments are large or small, public or private, the thoughts running through your mind may be along the same thread as mine: How did I get here? What happened to my life? What happened to my dreams? *Why am I not there yet?*

Looking through the twin prisms of reflection and perspective, I began to unravel my tangled situation. You may have done the same thing. My own Meltdown Moments are usually triggered by regret, fear, and uncertainty: what happened in the past; what is happening right now; what might happen in the future. Everyone's situations are unique, but they usually contain several common components. Our Meltdown Moments are really a twisted combo meal of life's issues.

Your Past

> *It was good for me to be afflicted
>   so that I might learn your decrees.* Psalm 119:71 (NIV)

While I was in the middle of the Meltdown Moment I described earlier, myriad images were flashing in my head: What was done to me. What I did to somebody else. The paths and opportunities I should have/would have/could have pursued. The people who brought joy and peace into my life. The people who left me crushed, brokenhearted, angry, and bitter. The years I let fear, distraction, loneliness, and procrastination steal my peace and abort my progress. The people I loved and lost. The people who died. The people who betrayed me. The people I betrayed. Everybody's got a past, and it's not always pretty. Mine certainly wasn't! Because of my own skewed self-image, I've made many bad decisions. I've done some things that I'm glad there wasn't a YouTube to document. Don't laugh: Some of you may have *been* on YouTube! Some may have been in prison. Some of us have financial failings, physical illnesses, addictions, or other health issues that challenge us even today. Some have been hamstrung by the way we view and handle ourselves and other people. Some have experienced life events that left us physically, emotionally, intellectually, morally, financially, and even spiritually bankrupt. Some of us have a divorce or two in our pasts. Or three.

But you know one good thing about our past? It's in the past—where it belongs! If (and in the words of my late grandmother, that's *if*) we choose to leave our pasts behind (admittedly, a continual process) instead of wallowing in them, they can remain behind us. Issues from past decisions may still affect us in the present, but we can choose not to be haunted by them. There is a major difference in learning from our mistakes and wallowing in them. You know another good thing? Every painful, blundering, even sinful action I have taken contained seeds of wisdom that can grow into a shade of safety (if I choose to allow it to). If you had done everything perfectly, you likely would not be open to the challenge of change and growth that brought you to this point. If I could change some things in my past, trust me, I would. But . . . perhaps if I had been "perfect," with few Meltdown Moments, I might have been prideful, and then taken full credit for my own successes. I certainly wouldn't appreciate the progress I have made to date. And I definitely wouldn't be writing this book!

Understand, God is not shocked by anything we have done, are doing, or will do. It's not as if He is sitting in Heaven, anthropomorphic Hand slapped against anthropomorphic Face, gasping Oh, My, Me! No, He knows the end from the beginning. We're the ones who don't know the plot twists and turns in our life's movie script.

We can't change our history. Some things we've done in our past affect us right now. But we don't have to live in the past. We can leave the land of regret and stop the revolving door of repetitive error. It's not easy. But it is possible. It's a process that starts with taking a clear, honest look at the events in our lives that contributed to our Meltdown Moments.

 **Purpose Point:**
Identify one part of your past that is on continual replay in the mp3 player of your memory.

Your Present

There's an oven commercial that follows a woman preparing for her first gourmet dinner party. In it, everywhere the hostess goes, from the market to her kitchen, she is shadowed by a black-clad, stuffy, NYC art-critic type who picks apart her every move: "Do [your guests] even *like* fish?" My personal Inner Critic is like that. He appears for the express purpose of impeding my progress. IC does not show up all the time, but when he does, he is *loud*! "No one wants to read your book. Your life certainly isn't perfect—why should anyone listen to you? You've attempted books before — you even erased one on your hard drive." Being a writer is already a form of emotional exhibitionism. Try working with an Inner Critic in your present. I have to keep duct tape around to silence him so I can get any work done and stay congruent.

As a man thinks in his heart, so is he. Proverbs 23:7 (NKJV)

This Proverbs passage opens with a situation in which a wealthy host is speaking positive words to his guest, but his thoughts are actually negative. The sociological term for this disconnect is called *incongruence*. Being incongruent is like driving forward in the car with the gear set to neutral. Eventually, you will slip into reverse — or blow out your engine. What gear is your life's "car" set to?

Our brains are really like little supercomputers. We have a wealth of thoughts to choose from each and every second. What we "host" determines our destiny. We can be incongruent in our words, our actions, and especially our thoughts. It's said that we create our own present. Look around you. What do you think about your life and the people in it? Everything we think about ourselves is reflected in our present circumstances. If they are not what we'd like, maybe the congruency isn't there. In other words, we can *say* that we want certain things to happen, but in actuality, as we work through the process of progress, we are running little programs (negative thought patterns, self-talk, and subsequent behavior based on our fears and beliefs) that negate our plans when we get into uncomfortable situations. Most, if not all, people have areas in their lives that are not congruent. When there is such disconnect between what we really believe and how we act, no wonder we have Meltdown Moments!

 **Purpose Point:**
Write down three thought patterns and behaviors in your life not congruent with your values, current interests, and God-given desires.

Your Fears

My worst fears have all come true. Job 3:25 (CEV)

When I was a kid, our church youth group went on an annual picnic outing to a local lake. The hot, sunny day was fun but uneventful. Then we started an afternoon softball game. One of the boys chased a stray fly ball into Lake Ray Hubbard—and never came out. He got caught in a sinkhole and drowned. The sight of Zachary, arms flailing in terror, was burned into my childhood memory from then on.

Fast forward a few years: I was a sophomore at my alma mater taking a mandatory swimming class. It was a fun, easy semester; we spent as much time wearing floaters and chatting with each other as we did actually swimming. Then it came time to earn a passing grade by swimming a single lap in the indoor competition pool. I had gone halfway down the lane and was circling back to the other end when I had a flashback of my childhood friend thrashing around in the water, screaming for help for the last time.

That's how your fears will follow you and trigger Meltdown Moments. I was assured of victory that day—until I was reminded of my fears. Here's another example:

Chapter One — Meltdown Moments

One snowy January morning, I stopped by my local supermarket to pick up sturdy apple cartons for moving. As I inched my way into the store to keep from slipping, I saw an older woman doing the same. Just as she reached me, out of nowhere she yelled out (and I hope you'll overlook her brusqueness):

"This is *crap!*"

Without so much as looking in my direction, she added these chilling words:

"To be old, broke, and alone."

The woman turned and walked into the store without another word. Who was she? What had happened to her? What was her current situation? What was running through her mind that made her say those words right then? How did she arrive at her Meltdown Moment?

The anonymous shopper spoke to my fears that morning. I bet she spoke to some of yours, too. *Is her present going to be my future?* It's a dangerous thing to reach the point where you believe you have little to live for. When we start to focus on our fears, featuring the negative aspects of our lives, questioning our own significance, our thoughts can lead us into incongruence, which leads straight into Meltdown Moments.

It sounds funny to be afraid of our future, but if we fear that our future will be negative, we just might sabotage our current efforts so we don't have to face possible failure.

When we're hurting, it's hard to find anything good about what we are trying to rise above. Sometimes in tough times, we can fear, like the woman at the supermarket, that our present is as good as it gets. That's a lie. Our fears don't have to be our future.

 **Purpose Point:**
Write down three of your biggest fears. Are you afraid of your past, your present, or your future? Write down what scares you about each fear and why.

Your Focus

I've taken many of the psychological personality profiles on the market. In Myers-Briggs terminology, I am a classic ENFP—an extrovert whose energy is fueled by the pregnant possibilities of life. I love a variety of choices and enjoy the selection process.. But what makes me *me* can also be my Achilles heel—without diligence, I can become overwhelmed and lose focus. Losing focus leads to an inability to concentrate on one thing at a time to completion. Add my fear triggers to that and you're looking at a scattered, frustrated, ineffective Charlotte Ann—a Meltdown Moment waiting to happen.

Part of the reason for our failures is broken focus. What we think about is where we focus. Where we focus is what we feed. What we feed is what grows in our lives. I can admit to having fed my thoughts with way too much attention to what other people thought about me, my life, and my goals. I granted others power over my self-esteem to the point where I fed myself negative self-talk. In other words, I let other people tell *me* how to feel about *me*. I also wasted precious time supporting and nurturing others' plans and dreams without taking the time to water my own. At the end of the day, they accomplished their goals, but mine were left withering on the vine. Sometimes, I let people into my personal space and confidence who had no benefit in my life and allowed their not-so-hidden agendas to supplant my God-given one. As a result of feeding the wrong things, I allowed my focus to be broken. My broken focus kept me stuck in my past. I deserve better – and so do you! To successfully leave our pasts, we have to make a conscious decision to begin the healing process from it. Then we can better focus our vision on our future. We'll begin walking through that continual process in the next chapter.

 **Purpose Point:**
Identify and write down key times of day, events, and life areas when your focus is broken. Especially note the entrance and exits of people. Do you see a pattern?

Your Surroundings

A clean desk is a sign of a sick mind. (Or at least, that's what most of us writers tell ourselves.) Conversely, a neat home can be the prelude to a relaxing evening. Personally, I like to walk into a beautiful, tastefully decorated, fragrant, well-lighted home and then sit down to a carefully prepared meal. It refreshes me and helps me unwind from a stressful day. Unfortunately, I don't have a personal assistant, cleaning service, or home chef to ensure that effect when I walk through the door. However, since I understand that orderly surroundings have a psychological impact, I do my best to have as many places as possible neat and orderly. Your surroundings do make a difference in your mood. A messy mind and messy surroundings are classic ingredients for Meltdown Moments.

Of course, when I talk about surroundings, I'm not just speaking of what gated community, housing project, or apartment complex we live in. I'm talking about where we spend our *exterior* and *interior* lives:

> **Exterior life**—That's the "open to the public" part of our lives, what people see when they see us day to day. What do people think about when they look at you? When introduced to you for the first time, what's the first impression they have? What do you do every day? Where do you live? Are you holding on to a home, a job, a habit or a relationship that is not consistent with where you want to be in the next phase of your life? Ask yourself these questions: When you look around your home and car, what do you see? What does your life look like? Do you have order in your physical surroundings? Does the music on your home, work, and car playlists inspire or agitate you? Do the people we frequently call, IM, Facebook, Google+ and text add peace or chaos to our lives? Whom do you go to lunch with? Whom do you confide in? What's the first thing you do upon waking up? The last thing you do at night?

Interior life—I'm talking about the part of your life that people *don't* see. We live our lives in our heads before we ever take any action. Everything we do begins with a thought. When you're alone with your thoughts, what do you think? Are you frustrated, fearful, or excited about your future? Are you praying? Whose voice do you listen to in your mind? What do you really think about yourself?

 **Purpose Point:**
Identify and write down three ways in which your interior and exterior surroundings contribute to your Meltdown Moments.

Your Connections

Can two walk together except they be agreed? Amos 3:3 (KJV)

A pastor friend of mine once advised me, "Periodically, it's good to go through your cell phone and hit the delete button!" He meant that purging your contact list of negative people is a good thing. The people we are connected to can bring us up—or down.

Remora People

There's a species of fish called *remoras* that live in warm-water climates. There are several species of remoras, but they all share certain characteristics: 1) they all have a circle of sucker-like fins on their head that they use to attach themselves to larger host fish like whales and sharks; 2) they all need the movement of the larger fish to survive (they can't live in stagnant water); and 3) they all feed off the leftovers of the larger fish. In other words, they take food, transportation, and protection from the host. Most remoras don't harm the host fish, but some do. Because they tend to attach in multiples, their weight hinders the host's speed in the water. Others damage their skin because their sucker is abrasive. One thing's for sure, they don't give anything back. That's the difference between attachments and connections; a two-way giving street vs. a one-way dead end.

I can attest to "remora people" in my own life. I have definitely allowed them to attach to me; in turn, they slowed down my progress. Some opened the door to some of my major Meltdown Moments. Let me be real, too: I've also been a "remora" who brought toxicity to other people's lives. I bet you can say the same thing. Sometimes people attach themselves to us, luring and detouring us with time thievery, discouragement, manipulation, and other negative behavior. Some use flattery and "appreciation" to earn their attachment. Sometimes we select them ourselves, and then embrace them into our hearts against our own better judgments. Like an e-mail virus, their bad influence replicates and does damage not only to our own lives, but sometimes even to the people who are actually connected to us.

Here's another spin on this concept: Some people are not bad to us, but are bad *for* us. They do bring us some value, but in exchange they extract a high price from us in extravagant loyalty to their lives and personal agendas. Some take a heavy toll in the drama and chaos surrounding their presence. Others are not necessarily bad for us but are headed in a different direction than where we would like to go in our own lives. Some well-meaning friends may caution against your Big Dream pursuit. Satisfied with their own lives, they don't understand why you aren't happy. Some folks are downright miserable but are unwilling to do the hard work it takes to change. Others simply don't want you to leave them behind. That's OK. Just realize up front that it will take all the energy you've got to change your own life. You have little energy to spare. The people who are truly your friends will celebrate you and your efforts. By the way, not everyone wants you to achieve your Big Dream at all. Not everyone spending time with you, smiling at you, is your friend. (We'll discuss some of those people in chapter 7.)

As we start to go further in our Big Dreams discussion, it's important to emphasize that our attachments and connections can make the difference between destiny and defeat.

 **Purpose Point:**
Write down three "remora people" in your life. Identify whether they're bad *to* you or bad *for* you and why.

The Common Denominator—Y.O.U.

> *A person without self-control is like a house with its doors and windows knocked out.*
> Proverbs 25:28 (MSG)

The common denominator is Y.O.U.—Your Own Universe. Y.O.U. encompasses our total set of past decisions, the fears that set us off, our present viewpoints, the distractions that break our daily focus, our surroundings, and the people and things we are attached and connected to. All of that and more have brought us to our Meltdown Moments.

Y.O.U.

The good news is, Your Own Universe can be reordered. You're not through yet! *If you have a pulse, you have a purpose.* Each new day is God's gracious gift to us. He gives us fresh opportunities to allow Him to reorder our lives. It's the closest thing to a do-over that we get in life!

Sometimes it seems that things will get worse—a lot worse—before they get better. In the next chapter, we'll discuss extended shadow seasons and how to get through them.

 *Power Point*
Celebrate the removal of one "remora" from your life.

A Prayer for You

Father, as we move forward through this book, I ask You to bring illumination, clarity, and healing to every person holding it. Walk with them as they fight their way out of Meltdown Moments. Speak to the heart of each person, drawing every one closer to You. Settle their spirits during their shadow seasons. Help them to ignore the outer voices and Inner Critics speaking doubt and downfall over their lives. Use the Purpose Points to shine light on the "why" behind their "what." Use each chapter's Reflective Questions to prompt readers to participate in their own transformation. With each chapter's Power Points, let them celebrate a milestone in their progress. Reveal and resurrect their Big Dreams as You prepare them for their purpose and destiny. In Your Son's name, Amen.

Reflective Questions

- How did you arrive at your Meltdown Moments?
- What is the source of your pain?
- What from your past have you taken into your present?
- Who or what have you allowed to break your focus? Why?
- What in Y.O.U. (Your Own Universe) needs to be removed, replaced, or reordered?

Shadow Seasons

Chapter 2

What do you do
When you've done all you can
And it seems like it's never enough?
And what do you say
When your friends turn away,
You're all alone?
Tell me, what do you give
When you've given your all
and seems like you can't make it through?

Donald "Donnie" McClurkin, *Stand*

My childhood classmate Willie Charles Lee was one of my closest friends and "road dogs." A curious mix of sensitive artist and athletic ladies' man, Charles and I shared a love for sporty cars, funky music, and jazzy clothes. He helped me move into my first apartment; I helped him get over his first great love. We shared secrets while eating Tex-Mex combo plates washed down with Coronas at the latest hole in the wall we'd discovered. We were both southpaws. Our twenty- and thirty-something conversations were filled with hope and promises of successful creative writing and graphic design careers. Charles and I owned one of those flexible friendships—we didn't have to see each other often to stay close.

Then, shortly after Christmas, my mom got a phone call: Charles had been running to catch the city bus for work, somehow went under the wheels, and was run over from the waist down. I was shocked and worried but not fearful. My buddy was a high school footballer, gym rat, and jogging enthusiast. If anyone would recover from an accident like this, it would be Charles. So I was stunned when I walked into his hospital room and saw him battered, immobile, and semi-conscious. Yet two days later, he seemed out of the woods. New Year's Day, I watched, amused, as Charles flirted with the nursing staff; then I scolded him as he playfully asked for candy (he had found out some time ago that he was a diabetic). I offered to buy Charles a set of weights as bait for him to work on his physical therapy. Then we prayed together—and he called me *his best friend*. He confided, "Charlotte, I'm worried about having a limp." I joked, "I'm worried about you having a *heartbeat!*" Little did I know it would come to just that.

Our visit together was the last time I saw him alive and alert. During successful follow-up surgery, Charles unexpectedly slipped into a coma and died two days later at the age of 39. The sharp brown wool suit he'd bought for an office Christmas party made a second appearance as his burial attire. Charles went into eternity—I plunged into a shadow season.

Shadow seasons are the long, cold winters of our emotional lives. If shadow seasons were presented in the form of a mathematical equation, it might look something like this:

>Life event(s)
>\+
>High level of importance
>−
>Effective ways to deal with life event
>\+
>Extreme impact on your life
>×
>Unrelenting stress
>=
>shadow season

Sometimes Meltdown Moments precede shadow seasons, sometimes not. Sometimes the seasons are triggered by mourning or a major life event. Other times, you slip into them without even fully realizing why.

Types of Shadow Seasons

Some shadow seasons happen suddenly. They drop on you like a flash flood. Others sneak up on you like a slight chill that eventually morphs into full-blown flu. Some only last a few weeks—others stretch into years. But they are often marked by sadness, fear, anxiety, and regret.

Visible Shadows

Some shadows are visible to everyone around you. When someone dies, people expect the family to go through an extended period of mourning. Emotionally tangible life events like job loss, death in a family, divorce, illness, loss of dreams, discovery of secrets are all understandable triggers for visible shadows. We instinctively understand and make allowances for people going through a visible shadow season.

Invisible Shadows

But there are also shadows that fall across your face for reasons unknown to anyone but you. Maybe not even you. What about the shadows you can't see? What do you do when everything "should" be going well, but really isn't? Some shadows stretch invisibly across seemingly successful lives. Everyone in your life considers your life to be fantastic—everyone except you. What's going on when the life you live is not the life you love?

Sunny Shadows

Sometimes it rains and the sun shines at the same time. Your life can be going so well in some areas and so poorly in others. How do you respond when you finally get that promotion at work—and your teenage daughter informs you she is pregnant? How can you celebrate when your doctor gives you a clean bill of health when in the same month, your father has been diagnosed with Alzheimer's?

How Shadow Seasons Feel

There's a drug commercial that poses the question: Where does depression hurt? Answer: Everywhere. Sounds like a description of a shadow season. People express themselves during shadow seasons in various ways: Some wear their feelings on their sleeves; others suffer quietly. Some begin to eat everything in sight; others barely pick up a fork. Some lash out at anyone unlucky enough to be in their paths. Some internally apologize for their very existence. Most feel like the way things are is the way things will always be. Sometimes you feel stuck in a moment you can't get out of.

Tear Tracks

Music legend Smokey Robinson told the story of how he wrote one of his iconic songs. He said he imagined someone crying so hard that the tears left tracks on his face. I relate to that, Mr. Robinson. I bet you can, too. Life can slap you down so many times that staying down seems like an attractive option. I know what it's like to feel I've been stoned and left for dead. I've been left so many times, I'm surprised when people stay. I've cried until my own hot tears left tracks on my face. Shadow seasons can feel like tear tracks on your heart.

 **Purpose Point:**
Stop and describe your current shadow season.
Is it internal or external? Visible or invisible?
Silent or sunny? How do you feel?

Internal Reactions

Regret

Regret is a long, questioning look back over your past actions. What if things had been different? What if I hadn't [fill in the blank]? Regret is a real part of being human, a self-activated emotion. It has paralyzed me. I have regretted ways I hurt others. I have regretted loving the wrong people. I have regretted not taking advantage of opportunities. No one lives a perfect life. But your life doesn't have to revolve around remembering and reliving the pain of your past. We'll discuss more positive options further in this chapter.

Fear

Fear, being afraid to face the future, is a major shadow season weapon. There are two major buckets of fear: 1) the fear of what *might* happen, and 2) the fear of what actually *will* happen as the result of our current situation. Neither of them can be totally accurate, because fear gives no room for God to move in our lives. He is the ultimate "game changer."

Paralysis

Fear plus regret can often lead to paralysis by analysis, which totally immobilizes our decision-making process: What if I make the wrong choice? What if I make the wrong choice—again? What if "they" don't like what I do? *What do I do now?* For fear of making the wrong choice, we make no choice at all. Making no decision keeps us stuck in our shadow seasons.

 **Purpose Point:**
What internal responses do you have right now? Regret? Fear? Paralysis? One we haven't discussed?

External Reactions

Blame

Blame makes other people more responsible for our lives than we are. We say things like "You just don't understand what he/she//they/it did to me. . . . You have no idea what kind of upbringing I had. . . . It's the economy/the job market/my family, etc. . . . I just can't catch a break." You may be right, to a degree. It may not have been your fault. Certain circumstances are definitely out of our control. But blaming others only makes us feel justified temporarily. It doesn't make our life better in the long run.

Rage

Some of us still rage out verbally (and some rage out physically) over events that happened to us years ago. The person(s) may be long gone from our lives or even dead, but we are still angry and bitter. Unfortunately, the people who are still in our lives wind up having to pay the penalty for what happened in our pasts. Sometimes we even rage out at people who have nothing to do with our situations at all! They simply happen to be in the wrong place at the wrong time and are forced to bear the brunt of our pain, shame, or frustration.

Fight

Sometimes we have to fight our way through shadow seasons. That isn't the same as fighting people. Sometimes we waste time with emotional shadowboxing, punching the air against invisible or unreachable opponents. Other times, we coast along, employing "rope-a-dope" techniques: leaning back against the ropes of life and taking the blows, instead of identifying, gathering and employing the proper tools to fight our way out.

Isolate

Animals often isolate when they are hurting. People do, too. When we are in a shadow season, it's often easier to hide from people and avoid painful situations rather than listen to well-meaning people telling you to simply snap out of it. It takes a lot of energy to continually explain yourself to people who won't understand anyway, or worse, to slap on a fake smile just to be sociable. When we are tired, lonely, scared, and hurting, sometimes it feels easier to stay at home and hide than to face our fears.

Purpose Point:
What external responses do you have to your shadow seasons? Blame? Rage? Fighting? Isolation? One we haven't discussed?

Walking Through Shadow Seasons

Yea, though I walk through the valley of the shadow of death, I will fear no evil.   Psalm 23:4 (KJV)

What I'm about to describe is a process. I already told you that walking through a shadow season takes everything we've got. Just remember, we're intent on walking through the season. We've already discussed what doesn't work; here's some insight into what does.

Stop
Whatever you are doing, wherever you are, right now, STOP. You have likely been spinning your wheels, worrying, working, trying to do everything you can to get off this treadmill on your own. Now, it's time to bring—and keep—God in the equation. Turn the computer off. Back away from the refrigerator. Don't hurt yourself. Take a deep breath. Calm yourself down. Right now, this minute, the world isn't coming to an end. Right now, this second, you are not starving. Right now, you are all right.

Assess
Take the time to see where you are in this moment. Assess your situation from all angles—spiritual, emotional, financial, whatever. I said assess, not obsess. What have you done so far to deal with your shadow season? How's that working for you?

 **Purpose Point:**
Assess your current or most recent shadow season. What have you learned about your own behavior?

For-Getting (For-Giving)

> *I do not consider myself yet to have taken hold of it. But one thing I do: Forgetting what is behind and straining toward what is ahead*   Philippians 3:13 (NIV)

I've been angry about being taken advantage of, abused, or taken for granted. I've also been ashamed at how my own actions have hurt or disappointed other people. But you know what? For me to move past my shadow seasons and prepare to access my Big Dreams, I've had to first give myself and other people the precious gift of forgiveness.

I'm here to tell you that for you to *get* where God is taking you, you have to for-give where you have been. I'm not talking about a quick fix: It's a continual process. Nor am I talking about pretending painful events didn't happen, or allowing abusive, toxic people to remain in your lift. Like a wound that heals from the inside out, there are layers of forgiveness.

Endure

> *And so, after he had patiently endured, [Abraham] obtained the promise.*   Hebrews 6:15 (KJV)

I understand that it feels like you will never get through this. But feeling is not always reality. God promises to be with us and for us. Endurance, hanging in there even when we don't see the outcome yet, imparts a gradual toughness and inner strength that comes from walking with and waiting on God. No night, even the longest ones, lasts forever.

Trust

You are not the sum of your shadows. Let me say that again: *You are not the sum of your shadows.* I don't care what happened, how it happened, or to whom it happened, understand that God loves us and wants to bring His best into our lives. Let's trust Him for that.

Even if we don't know how it's going to happen. Even if we don't know when it's going to happen. Even if we don't feel like it's going to happen at all.

Yield

Even Jesus had to yield to God's will. In the Garden of Gethsemane, He prayed: "Let this cup pass from me" (Matthew 26:39, KJV). When we yield to God and acknowledge His sovereignty over our situation, He corrects our character flaws and shapes our character.

Chronic Shadows

The trying of your faith worketh patience. James 1:3 (KJV)

Now, I've got to acknowledge that some shadows take a lifetime to walk through. Not everything goes away immediately with a prayer, a pause, and a quick praise. The apostle Paul mentioned an affliction that he prayed unsuccessfully three times to be free from. Paul concluded that the reason for his affliction was to bring humility to counterbalance his incredible divine revelations. Talk to people who suddenly succeed after years of struggling. They will likely tell you that a part of them is always looking over their shoulder, planning and plotting, scrimping and saving, "just in case something happens." That's a chronic fear shadow. Chronic shadows are truly trying, and they force us to rely on God in a way that maybe we wouldn't have had it not been for their presence in our lives.

What Do You Do When the Problem Is You?

And Nathan said to David, Thou art the man.
2 Samuel 12:7 (KJV)

What do you do when your shadow season was of your own (un)doing? What do you do when your Meltdown Moments weren't the result of "what happened to me?" What do you do when it's your fault? What do you do when it's true what "they" said about you? When you alone are to blame for consistently making spectacularly bad decisions that affected not just yourself, but your friends, your children, your spouse, your health, your finances, and your connections? Did you create a selfish, "all about me" lifestyle that crushed everyone that stood in your path, leaving you alone to celebrate your hollow successes? King David had to deal with the consequences of his own bad actions. Although he had access to plenty of beautiful women to choose from legally, he took Bathsheba to his bed. Then he ordered her husband, the loyal soldier Uriah, killed in the front line of battle. David hastily married the grieving widow to conceal the fact that he had impregnated another man's wife.

God sent a messenger to call King David out. At God's command, the prophet Nathan risked his own life to tell the truth. You see, a king so wrapped up in his own wrongdoing that he would kill his own faithful soldier might have no problem killing the person who dared to tell him he was wrong to do so.

As the story unfolds in 2 Samuel 12, according to Nathan's dire prophecy, the baby born to David and Bathsheba became deathly ill. King David fasted and lay on the floor, asking mercy on his newborn's life. But God had spoken. When David learned of the child's death, he did five things that are a template for our own restoration in shadow seasons.

He got up. The mighty king had sunk as low as he could get: lies, adultery, pregnancy, murder, and involuntary infanticide—all in one situation. He had created a deadly shadow season for himself, Bathsheba, *and* their baby. David lay face down on the dirty palace floor, begging God for the life of his innocent child. He was continually reminded of his own sinful selfishness, which had caused this mess in the first place. But once King David realized that the child had indeed died according to Nathan's prophecy, he got up. He didn't stay on the ground; he didn't keep begging; he didn't keep beating himself up.

What's done is done. We can't move into our purpose and destinies and stay in a shadow season at the same time. Whether it was our fault, someone else's fault, or no fault, it takes a conscious act of faith to get up and begin the healing process. Getting up does not involve your ability alone as much as it does God's. Take a leap of faith and believe that He will strengthen and empower you as you make the effort to get up.

He washed himself. David had to remove his garments of mourning and wash off the clay reminder of his failure.

Everyone feels fresher and cleaner after a bath or shower. Dirt has no place in our Big Dreams. Prayer, praise, and meditation on the Word of God help facilitate the cleansing process that keeps you from carrying your past into your future. Start with Psalm 23. Reflect on how much God cares for you. Read Jeremiah 29:11. Understand that God's plan for us is better than anything we can cook up for ourselves.

He anointed himself. It wasn't enough to wash himself. King David had to give his olfactory senses something to focus on. He anointed himself because he had been anointed to be king.

By anointing, I mean the cleansing, healing, and renewing of our spirits that comes from spending time in prayer and communion with God. A good fragrance identifies with the wearer. Our "emotional fragrance" is how others read us before we open our mouths. A positive emotional fragrance precedes us into a room. Moving out of your shadow seasons requires more than a quick spiritual dab behind the ears.

He changed his clothes. A little black dress and stilettos have no place at a picnic. A change in clothes indicates a change of occasion. David had to move out of mourning. The season had changed. God's will had prevailed.

For me, "changing clothes" meant that I had to cut ties with some people completely, whether the other person liked it or not (There have been people who have had to cut ties with me as well.) If we are tied to people, places, and habits that lock us into our shadow seasons, the process of changing our clothes must begin. We'll talk more about cutting out toxic people and situations in chapter 3.

He worshipped. King David was called "a man after [God's] own heart" (Acts 13:22, NIV) because he understood one key thing: how to worship and connect with God, even in his shadow seasons. He worshipped even when acknowledging his own wrongdoing. He worshipped God even when his child died. He worshipped God by acknowledging that He is great and sovereign and still loves us.

Understand that whatever happens in our lives, even the most painful things, will ultimately be used to mold our character and bring correction, direction, guidance, and fruitfulness to our lives. God loves us no matter what. He promises to work things out for our good (Romans 8:28), no matter what things look like initially. Because He is God, the only one powerful enough to heal our situations, He is worthy of worship, no matter what the circumstance.

The Wounded Worshipper

No matter how spiritual we may consider ourselves, even though "The Word works," even though we quote Scriptures, go on prayer walks, and recite affirmations, there are times when most of us, even Christians, will find ourselves among the walking wounded. We smile on the outside to cover up crushed, broken hearts. When that happens, the only thing left to do is worship the God Who can either bring us out or bring us through. It's only in worship that you get a connection to God.

My most soothing times in my own shadow seasons have been when I replaced the dirt of defeat with the water of worship. God is still God. When I'm spending too much time in the shadows, I start becoming fearful, obsessive, regretful, scattered, and ultimately ineffective. God does not love me any less by allowing my shadow seasons. I worship Him to acknowledge His love, His care, and His ability to work things out and bring me through.

King David got up from his shadow season. After mourning his own frailties and proclivities and sin and its horrific results, he washed himself, changed his clothes, and worshipped the God Who is still worthy of worship.

David's wounded worshipping got God's attention. The next son born to David and Bathsheba, now referred to in the biblical text as his wife, was the person we know as King Solomon. But Solomon had another name first: Jedidiah, which means "beloved of God." God may allow wounding to bring character into your life, but He does not stop loving you. You are still beloved to Him. And you still have purpose.

 *Power Point*

Take a moment and celebrate God's love, forgiveness and presence, even in tough times.

Then take a moment and forgive yourself.

The Secrets of the Shadows

Sometimes it feels like we've been standing in the shadows of loneliness and disappointment for our entire lives. Even our successes can seem like dim lights compared to the spotlights of others' spectacular achievements. But I've learned some shadow secrets: Shadows have *purpose*. They provide shade, identification, and protection from danger.

Here's another secret: Shadows have *power*. It's easy to trust God in the sunny times. But try continuing to walk, head held high, trusting Him when all hell is breaking loose. When we spend portions of our lives undercover, secluded away from prying eyes and critical tongues that can wound and wither, we learn what's real and what's fake. We learn how to watch, fight, and feed our spirits in prayer. We learn how to follow truth no matter what. God has a way of putting us in shadow situations where we have no choice but to trust Him. Here are some other secrets of our S.H.A.D.O.W.S. to consider:

Suffering and Solitude—People don't like to talk about suffering, let alone experience it. But God brings us closer to Him during times when we are in physical and emotional pain in a way that we wouldn't experience otherwise. Suffering in the shadows, especially when we don't know where God is and can't feel Him around, forces us to rely on faith that He is still connected to us. That's because true suffering strips away the unimportant. Anyone who has spent time in a hospital knows what I'm talking about. Suffering drives away people who are only attached to you when things are going well. Suffering draws out people who are assigned to minister to you. Some of the people who appear in either category may surprise you. When we come out of a season of suffering, we appreciate the good times that much more.

Solitude doesn't seem like it fits in the "benefit column" of shadow seasons either. But those of us accustomed to the cacophony of our Inner Critics and external voices offering bad advice and unwise counsel understand that solitude—with God—can indeed be a weapon and an asset. Stretches of solitude with God (as opposed to isolation with just ourselves) teach us what we're made of. Some of us would never grow if it weren't for the shadows. My friend and assistant, Dawn, gave me a beautiful plant recently. Knowing that I am far from the gardener she is, she pointed out that this plant requires lots of sun and water. In other words, it would be difficult for even me to drown and fry it! But some plants grow and thrive in the cool evening shadows. Night-blooming jasmine emits its fragrance to help you find it. In the shadows of solitude, we learn what fragrances we have been blessed to release to the world.

Healing—I know we just talked about suffering, but the healing you need may not be physical. It may be emotional, financial, and especially spiritual. During shadow seasons, God, through His Word, will speak and release a balm of healing to your soul. You can move out of your shadows a healthier, more whole, balanced, stronger person.

Anointing—It was customary in hot climates to anoint the body with oil to protect it from excessive perspiration. When mixed with perfume, the oil imparted a delightfully refreshing and invigorating sensation. Athletes anointed their bodies as a matter of course before running a race. As the body, anointed with oil, was refreshed, invigorated, and better fitted for action, so the Lord would anoint His "sheep" with the Holy Spirit, Whom oil symbolizes, to fit them to engage more freely in His service and run in the way He directs—in heavenly fellowship with Him.

Direction—Plants and seeds come with directions on their containers. When they arrive in the garden, they are plunged into darkness and dirt. No one sees it happening, but the plants develop a root system that will sustain them. The ground around them is weeded and fertilized, protected from predators, and nurtured to create a healthy environment. Some vine plants are even trained by sticks and ropes to hold them up during seasons of growth and preparation. In the appropriate time, they are ready to yield the most fruit. During shadow seasons, God gives us direction on how to prepare to break through to the next level in our lives. While He's directing, guiding, and even correcting us, He protects us from predators. He guides us to be our best through the use of what seem like restrictions and barriers. He teaches us how to create and function in a healthy environment. When we finally break through our shadow season, we are ready to yield fruit that will not only sustain ourselves and others, but bring glory to Him.

Overcoming Power—In shadow boxing, the trainer teaches technique, accuracy, and stamina. We learn how to flex our muscles in the shadows. We learn how to bob, weave, and jab our opponent. Boxers learn the components for victory before they ever step into the ring. In the shadows, we learn the discipline it takes to overcome adversity.

Wisdom—Never say what you will or won't do in a situation. We learn more about ourselves and others when we go through the shadows than we ever learn in the good times. Sometimes God will have us face our fears not to scare us, but to teach us how not to succumb to them. We learn how to handle our "kryptonite" in the shadows. Show Him what you've got!

Sustenance—God can be revealed to us as Jehovah-jireh, our Provider, in a whole new level in the shadows. He delights in showing His provisional excellence when no one is looking and when nothing seems to be working. There were instances when Jesus performed miracles and directed the recipient not to tell anyone. I have received provision and sustenance from God in ways so fantastic that I can't even tell people about them yet. During our life journeys, God gives us periods of rest, refuge, and renewal. Some of those times are disguised as shadow seasons.

What I Know about Shadows

With all due acknowledgments to Oprah Winfrey, this is what I know for sure: God wastes nothing, including shadow seasons. Example: I had been sitting on *Preserved for a Purpose*, incubating it, praying, and waiting for years. I had a title in my head. I formed an outline, worked on chapters here and there, even registered the book's domain name. However, I experienced no real, quick progress.

Then, a few years ago, a wealthy client hired me to do a book project. I was enthusiastic. I was committed. I was motivated at the potential financial reward on the back end of the deal. I assembled the team. I worked harder than I ever have for the longest sustained period of my life. Twelve- to fifteen-hour days, six and a half days a week, sacrificing my sleep, my ministry, my church, my family. I even worked for free for a period. In the end, the project went sour. I was devastated, brokenhearted, and I drifted into a bitterly cold shadow season.

Fast forward a year. After I had a milestone birthday party, God changed everything about *Preserved for a Purpose*: the title, the approach, the cover, the content. This is what I mean by God not wasting anything: The writing discipline I developed and the business practices I learned with that old project have helped me immensely in preparing this book for you.

It sounds like a silly realization, but I learned that God didn't stop providing for me when one business deal went bad. The truest thing I learned from that shadow season is something I spoke out of my own mouth. "As hard as I worked for you," I told my client, "I can work that hard for myself." And I did. Looking back, I can admit that I saw my client as a source instead of looking to God as the Source. God will block what seems like a sure thing so that He can give you His best instead. If I had continued down the path I was on, I would have settled for the crumbs from another person's table, when God wanted to gift me with my own cake. On my own table. I told you, shadow seasons have a purpose.

Preserved for a Purpose

I believe God orchestrates events, circumstances, and connections in a way that will, if we choose to follow Him, turn into our ultimate good. In the meantime, one of the biggest struggles in watching, working, and walking through shadow seasons in the late summer of life is waiting your turn. Likely you've had to celebrate other people's fruitfulness while you struggle with your own barrenness. Many of us have had to smile through our tear tracks. We've celebrated other people's new jobs, new homes, new cars, new marriages, new babies, new grandbabies, new friendships, growing businesses and ministries. We've applauded outwardly while wounded inwardly, wondering, *When will it be my time?*

But there's a blessing in the middle of the barrenness. The blessing is the peace that comes from developing complete and total trust in Him. One of the most powerful prayers I've prayed is "Father, do for me what I can't do for myself." (Truthfully, that includes everything, doesn't it?) The key is in the first part of the Lord's Prayer: Which art in heaven. His heavenly perspective is perfect. Simple acknowledgement of His sovereignty brings the freedom to trust Him when, how, and even if He answers.

Timing Is Everything

To be clear: When I talk about being preserved for a purpose, I'm not talking about totally orchestrating your own life. I didn't call this book, *Twenty-five Quick Sure-Fire Steps to Complete and Total Success* or some such nonsense. Psalm 37:4 reads, "Delight yourself in the LORD [first] and He will give you the desires of your heart." The idea is not one of a "Lotto Jesus." The concept is that you want what He wants, and He plants in you His desire for your highest good. If you tune in to Him, you will start to want what He wants. Then, in His timing, He gives you what you want—which is what He wants. The desires of your heart become not your selfish desires, but His desires for you. Beginning to sync with the flow of His will brings peace, purpose, and direction.

Now, I'm not totally there yet. And I can't estimate for you how long the process will take. There are some things I've been waiting on for more than 20 years. But I can tell you this: While I was waiting for God to move on some things, He was waiting for my character to develop, my confidence to blossom, my discipline to take root, and my leadership and decision-making skills to improve before

He could bless me with them. I can also tell you with confidence that if I had received some of what I thought I *should* have had by now, I would have definitely messed them up. Most important, He was waiting for my relationship with Him to grow so I could learn to trust Him even when I didn't immediately see how things were going to turn out. The deepest growth in my relationship with God has come in the times when I didn't feel Him. I've learned to treasure my time in the shadows, and so can you.

My friend Charles was talented, handsome, artistic, athletic, and brimming with purpose. Yet God chose to take him. If I have been blessed to live this long, I ought to *do something* with the time I have been given! I have been preserved for a purpose. So have you. Do something with it! Get up! Don't let your shadow season stop your destiny.

A Prayer for You

Father, I ask you to walk with each person through their Shadow Season, whether silent, sunny, chronic, or otherwise. Let the warmth of Your love replace the chill of uncertain times. Grant them peace. In Your Son's name, Amen.

Reflective Questions

- Can you see ways in which you might have been responsible for your shadow seasons?

- What triggers your negative—and positive—shadow season reactions?

- What have you learned about yourself in your shadow seasons? What have you learned about God?

- What and whom do you need to for-get to for-give?

- What purpose do you believe you have been preserved for?

Chapter Three — Site Planning

Site Planning

Chapter 3

Where there is no vision, the people perish.
Proverbs 29:18 (KJV)

Have you ever walked into a store on a rainy morning and spotted a colorful display of umbrellas by the front door? That's not because the store managers are clairvoyant. It's not because the store personnel pores over the weather segment of the news. It's because the management depends on the fact that *most people generally don't plan.*

People don't plan for a number of reasons. Sometimes, we're afraid of being let down if things don't work out in our favor. Sometimes, we lack discipline to put things down on paper or in our computers. Sometimes, under the guise of being "spiritual," we claim that God will "order our steps." That is true—but we have to actually be *making* steps for them to be ordered!

Planning is also critical for a building to be constructed properly. Before a skyscraper is built, the architects meet and do what is called *site planning*. The site-planning process creates the blueprint for the entire building project. After the blueprint is made, the plans are submitted to a city manager or other public officials for approval. Sometimes plans are modified before the actual construction is started. Planning can be the difference between success and failure.

But before even a line is drawn on a blueprint, the building was a gleam in a visionary's eye. This person may not have been an architect—but he or she did have a Big Dream. Our site-planning process starts with seeking God for our Big Dream. Our prayer process and the work we have done so far will start to unfold and expose it to us. We're going to follow a building metaphor over the next few chapters to illustrate the process of beginning the work of building our Big Dreams. Let's put on our hard hats and get going!

Dare to Dream

The Big Dream is a distillation of your future. It encompasses the purpose you have been preserved for. It's that dream you stayed in the shadows all these years waiting for. You may have children, a spouse, a job, or serve in some leadership capacity in your life. You may have past great accomplishments. Certainly, those things intersect with what I am talking about. But I'm speaking of what you're about to do *now*. The Big Dream is that thing you can't do without. It's the thing you don't want to die without doing—or that person you don't want to die without becoming. When God gives you a Big Dream, it's bigger than anything else you could imagine. If it doesn't scare you to death, it's probably not a Big Dream. If you can easily forget about it, it's not a Big Dream. If people can talk you out of it, it's definitely not a Big Dream. It doesn't have to be winning the Nobel Peace Prize. It can be as personal as committing to help raise your new grandchild to adulthood, no matter what it takes. Your Big Dream speaks to the dormant passion within you.

Dare to dream. Others want you to reduce your dreams to fit their reality. God wants you to expand your reality to fit your Big Dream. Enlarge the tents of your imagination and creativity. *Think big!*

Defining Your Dream

If you look for it, there is always something that piques your passion. Dare to dream the Big Dream, even at 40, 50, 60, 70, and beyond.

Your Big Dream has defining characteristics. Here's a "short list" for you to think about:

> Your Big Dream *connects* some people to you.
>
> Your Big Dream *subtracts* some people from your life.
>
> Your Big Dream *cuts* unnecessary attachments.
>
> Your Big Dream *multiplies* the favor of God on your life.
>
> Your Big Dream *divides* people's opinions of you.
>
> Your Big Dream *eliminates* unnecessary activities from your life.
>
> Your Big Dream *establishes* order in Y.O.U.
>
> Your Big Dream *restores* people to wholeness—starting with yourself.

Your Big Dream *heals* people's hearts, minds, and spirits.

Your Big Dream *elevates* people to their rightful place in life.

Your Big Dream *will draw enemies*.

Your Big Dream *blesses* other people.

Your Big Dream *ignites* other people.

Your Big Dream *attracts* attention—both positive and negative.

Your Big Dream *requires* big faith.

Your Big Dream *will bless you* in ways you never imagined.

You are the *"pastor"/leader/guardian* of your Big Dream.

Your Big Dream will likely *outlive* you.

Your Big Dream *shapes* your present and powers you into your future.

Your Big Dream "changes the game" of your life.

Your Big Dream makes *YOU a game changer.*

 **Purpose Point:**
Using this list, write down five attributes of your Big Dream. Why did you select them? How do you feel about them?

Follow Your Favor

How do you know you are on the path to your Big Dream? Sooner or later, favor follows Big Dreams. Once you begin, you will find favor to accomplish it. For the purposes of this book, I define **favor** as the following:

Specific, focused awareness, observation, and assistance from others that helps you to accomplish your purpose.

You won't see favor for your Big Dream until you set out on the path to seek it. Remember, favor is about more than you and your "moment on stage." It's about the other people whose very lives are dependent on your Big Dream.

 **Power Point**

Get happy! Your life is about to change for the better.

The View from the Vision

Write the vision. Habakkuk 2:2 (KJV)

Have you ever heard someone say, "I'm living the dream"? They mean they are experiencing an ideal life that others only dream about. Take a few moments and imagine yourself living your Big Dream. The following exercise is about developing and keeping a vision for your new life. Feel free to add your own questions as you think of them. Be sure to capture your Big Dream on paper or on computer.

First of all, have you given yourself permission to live your Big Dream? Do you truly believe you belong there? Can you play the movie of your new life in your mind without stopping, or does the mental film come to a screeching halt with imaginary roadblocks? Henry Ford put it this way: "Whether you think you can or you think you can't, you're right."

How do you look in your Big Dream? What is distinctive about your appearance? What do you wear every day? Is your wardrobe dressy, casual, business related, or a combination? What do you drive? A sporty convertible, a truck, a family-sized sedan or SUV, or perhaps a bus that assists you in your life? Do you work at home, in an office or store, or do you work onsite and telecommute? Where do you worship?

Who's sharing your Big Dream with you? If you're single and would like to be married, imagine life with your new spouse. Have you made time and room in your life, heart and world for him or her? Have you made the necessary emotional cuts from your past? If you're married, are you and your spouse on the same page about accomplishing your Big Dream? If not, how are you going to get them there?

Think of where you'd like to live your Big Dream. Is your home base a gated community, a high-rise condominium, or a cozy suburb? Drive to the location. Make an appointment to tour one of the places you'd like to live in. Do you prefer one-story or two-story homes? Brick, frame, or stucco? Is your home base near a school, church, or shops that you like?

Is your Big Dream starting a new business, ministry, or nonprofit? In what capacity do you serve? Does your Big Dream involving serving others in a different cultural environment than the one you live in? Pick up magazines and surf the Internet to learn about the needs, issues, and interests of the people there. Better yet, spend time with the people you hope to serve. Find out their needs, fears, hopes, and desires. Don't simply invite them to your base of operations. (If you can't help them in some way, it's not really ministry.) Spend time with them in their own environment. Jesus spent time with people at places other than the temple, for example, at dinner, at a wedding, at the lake, and so on. What about inviting them to dinner at your home?

Finally, once you've achieved your Big Dream, will you operate in humility? Who will benefit from your Big Dream other than yourself? Whom are you helping right now? Do you fully understand that a Big Dream is bigger than you "getting yours"?

Purpose Point:
Schedule one field trip to your Big Dream (library, Internet, city) to learn about what it might be like. What in your current life reflects how you want to live then?

The Power of Possibility

With God, all things are possible. Matthew 19:26 (KJV)

God minds His own business. From the beginning of recorded time, Elohim has been known for making something out of nothing. His signature modus operandi is to *speak*. He opened His triune mouth and light sprang out of darkness. Elohim spoke and the worlds were framed into existence. He speaks and gives the elements a name. He speaks and all of creation comes into existence. He taught mankind the principle of speaking things into existence. This principle, introduced in the book of Genesis, continued in Jesus' teachings. There are multiple passages in which Jesus emphasized the power of possibility. Mark 11:13 (AMP) illustrates one of them:

> *Truly I tell you, whoever says to this mountain, Be lifted up and thrown into the sea! and does not doubt at all in his heart but believes that what he says will take place, it will be done for him.*

 **Purpose Point:**
If you knew for sure that what you spoke in faith would, instantly or eventually, come into existence, what would you say? Practice saying it right now.

Clarifying Your Big Dream

By now, I'm sure you've been thinking a lot about your Big Dream. In our last church leadership retreat, I used vision boards to engage participants in the vision-casting process. I went to IKEA and picked up some inexpensive framed corkboard. Then I asked participants to take the stack of magazines and newspapers I provided to create a vision of the life they wanted to lead. This included spiritual, family, work, educational, personal, and financial aspects and more. The vision board helped them clarify the vision in their minds.

 **Purpose Point:**
Pick up an inexpensive corkboard, some push pins, and a few magazines. Then begin to bring your Big Dream to life before your eyes. What are the first five items that go on your board?

Develop Your Vision

In the book of Esther, the beautiful Hebrew maiden was crowned queen after a 12-month preparation period. Hadassah (before she was renamed Esther) was subjected to six months of myrrh treatment and six months with perfume and other spices. Then, after preparation, she was submitted for consideration. King Xerxes delighted in her and selected her as queen over all of his far-reaching empire.

Some of you are going places you never dreamed you would go. But it's time to get prepared and start setting order into your world *now*. Take the time to develop your vision before exposing it to the world. It's exciting to share your enthusiasm, but proper timing is critical. Remember when we talked about the underground plant in chapter 2? You don't dig up a plant every few days to show off its progress. Give your Big Dream the gift of preparation. Esther learned the protocol of the palace long before she was promoted. Learn the protocol of your "palace." You never know when the King will call you into service.

Ordering Your Vision

Ordering your vision is a process. We talked about developing your vision. Ordering your vision involves setting things in order *now* that are needed to maintain your Big Dream when you achieve it. We shouldn't wait till we see progress to start working. Too many times we visit our Big Dream in our minds but fail to prepare to move in permanently.

A money book author wrote about how one group of people finds their entertainment outside the house, while another creates their entertainment inside the house. For example, one family may spend money each weekend on movie tickets and expensive restaurants. They purchase expensive clothes just to make themselves appear prosperous. On special occasions, they may even rent an expensive car. On the other hand, another family lives very simply until they are financially set. Then they may purchase a house complete with media room and a game room, and then decorate each living area one by one. If it takes five years to fill and decorate the house, so be it. When they eventually finish, they own the house and everything in it. One family has temporary comfort; another has built comfort into their lifestyle. One visits their Big Dream; the other lives it. The difference between the two involves establishing the daily order required to stay where you'd like to be. We want to possess our Big Dream—not simply vacation there. We'll go through further steps for establishing order in our lives in chapter 4.

The Power of Risk (Fighting Fear)

I do realize that the path we are setting on is very scary. We are charting unfamiliar territory. It's almost like a game show in which you don't know for sure exactly what the prize will be—only the one you expect it to be. A really good game show highlights the tension between reward and risk. "Do you want what's behind door number 1, 2, or 3?" "Is that your final answer?" "If you guess the amount of the prize package . . ." "Open the case!" Sometimes we can be so fearful of a negative outcome that we never consider that the outcome could indeed be positive. Let's start to wrap our heads around the idea of actually achieving our Big Dreams. The best antidote to fear is to take steps even when we don't have a clue how everything will turn out.

The Five Questions

A vision without a target is like a race without a finish line. Here are five questions that will help you clarify your Big Dream:

1. **Who are you?** How do you define yourself? Not what you do, where you work, or who you are married to. When you describe you, what do you say? What makes you *you*? There's a reason they call it *self-esteem*. It's how you feel about you!

2. **Why are you here?** What purpose does your life serve? Hint: "Nothing" is not the correct answer. Someone is waiting for your presence in his or her life.

3. **What do you need?** Maslow's Hierarchy of Needs says all peoples' needs fall into the same general buckets: food, safety, love, esteem, and purpose (self-actualization). What do you need?

4. **What do you have to offer?** There's something you have to offer the world that no one can present but you. Like the simple slice of white bread on this book's cover, no gift is too small or too simple. What do you have to offer? In what area? In business? Personal relationships? Ministry or charity work? To what group of people will you offer your gifts? What is the thing you possess that if everything else went away tomorrow, you would want to remain, and why?

5. What are you committed to? What do you focus your life efforts on? What are you willing to die for? Who are you devoted to? Why are you committed? What in your life reflects that commitment?

 **Purpose Point:**
Stop right now and answer the five questions we just discussed in detail.

Before You Build

Count the Cost

When you make a decision to pursue your Big Dream, be prepared to pay the price in loneliness, ridicule, hanging on to faith in what you can't see currently, and even being ignored. Have you ever been around someone who acted like they knew you only when no one more "important" was around? During the planning stages, your Big Dream will likely attract attention from only a few people. Are you willing to pay the price?

And understand up front: There is a cost even when you start to "win." We'll talk about the Haters, Waiters, and Gators in Chapter 7.

Know that there will be tough times and setbacks in pursuit of your Big Dream. Just as a rainy season may cause a delay in construction, sometimes the rainy seasons of our lives may cause delays in progress. But don't worry—the sun *will* shine again.

Check the Code

The Word of God is the only code we can rely on. Jesus said in

Luke 6:47 (MSG): "These words I speak to you are not mere additions to your life, homeowner improvements to your standard of living. They are foundation words, words to build a life on." Remember, when tough times hit, the strength of your foundation and construction determines the reliability of your building.

Check the Materials
Several of my friends have built homes, and they tell me that one stud makes a difference. The integrity of the materials defines the value of the structure. One couple recently caused their sales clerk to be fired because he promised the moon but could deliver only moonbeams. We'll talk more about Building Materials in chapter 5.

Check Your Permit
I had a pastor friend who was forced to consider legal action against a person who had advised him that they could build a new parking lot for him but hadn't even gotten approval from their city. Do you have permission from God to do this? Check the manual before you begin: the Word of God, the Bible. After that, I sometimes refer to inspirational and motivational materials (online and print) that help me work effectively to address my challenges, build (and enjoy!) my Big Dream, and help it to affect more people. I've listed some of my library favorites in the back of this book.

What's in Your House?

At the church I founded, Eternal Springs Church Ministries, our slogan is "Security, identity, and wholeness in Him and Him alone." When I speak about building a "house" in this book, I'm not simply talking about your church. I'm also talking about your family, your community, your business, or simply *yourself*. The principles of security, identity, and wholeness still apply.

Security. When a baby is born, he or she doesn't look like much, just one big wrinkly, mewing ball of helplessness. All newborns do is cry, poop, and sleep! That's why mamas swaddle their babies, to help them feel secure in their environment. Don't expect people to be bowled over by your Big Dream. It doesn't look like much right now. Find your security in the fact that God gave it to you.

Identity. The second thing a family does is encourage the baby to recognize the surroundings. Mama, Daddy, nose, eye, ear, brother, sister. . . . Babies start to take on the appearance of their parents around that time too. The hair gets darker or lighter or curlier or straighter. That's what the second stage of building is like. As our Big Dream grows, it starts to take shape and become identifiable. Be careful what you call your Big Dream in its early stage. "My little . . . this old . . . my fantasy idea. . . .if I do this….I'm trying to…" Guard your speech against negativity, especially in the early stages. How you value your Big Dream now will dictate how others respond to it later.

Wholeness. Have you ever seen a 22-year-old sitting in a high chair? If you did, it was a sign that the person was developmentally disabled. As you work toward your Big Dream, you will begin to learn things about God and yourself that will help you to grow beyond where you were when you first started. Your life will become more whole and healed as you continue to develop it. It really is about the journey, not just the destination.

Fueling Your Future

In chapter 4, we'll discuss in detail how to add order to our world. We're going to deal with our perspective, self-image, health, time, finances, surroundings, and connections. As we move forward, I want you to start believing that your Big Dream will come to pass. With each step you make, start to expect things to happen.

A Prayer for You

Father, thank You for the courage, insight and wisdom necessary to lay the foundation for our Big Dreams. We receive the spirit of expectancy that You will give and reveal to us just what we need to accomplish them. As we plan, we believe the foundation is firm and laid out in partnership with You. Help us to clarify our visions and follow our favor in faith. In Your Son's name, Amen.

Reflective Questions

- Why is your Big Dream important to you?
- Are you willing to give your dreams to God and let Him give you the Big Dream?
- How do the answers to the Five Questions help you better understand your Big Dream?
- Do you believe in your Big Dream?

Part Two

Go Get Your Life Back

I know that you invested a lot
The return has been slow
You throw up your hands and say I give up
I just can't take it anymore
But I hear the Spirit say
That it's your time, the wait is over
Walk into your season

Donald Lawrence, *Seasons*

Laying Your Foundation

Chapter 4

And the Lord said to him, What is that in your hand?
Exodus 4:2 (AMP)

Once we've completed the site planning for our Big Dreams, it's time for the foundation to be laid. The first step in putting together the foundation is excavation. This is the longest part in the process. Anything of stability has to go deep before it goes high. I'm speaking of putting our lives in order so that we can get ready to build our Big Dreams. Let's talk about two categories of excavation:

Internal Excavation—My friend John Checki Jr. calls this "getting out of your own way." It's time to start getting your mind prepared for the journey ahead by making a conscious decision to devote each day to the realization of your Big Dream.

External Excavation—This involves adding order to our world so that we can function efficiently and effectively. We're going to walk some of these steps together later in this chapter.

Order Your Mind

> *Be transformed by the renewing of your mind.*
> Romans 12:2 (NKJV)

Your mind is the most powerful computer you will ever use. To start doing things differently, you have to start with thinking differently.

One of the first steps I implemented in reordering my mind was the elimination of the word "try." Try is a verbal loophole. Although the word can describe effort, it can also provide us with an exit strategy if what we are hoping for and talking about doesn't come to pass—or if we don't exert more effort. So I announced that I was eliminating it from my vocabulary. Then, I started correcting myself when the word slipped out of my mouth. I even corrected the people I mentor during teaching moments. That helped reinforce my own behavior. Gradually, I've become more successful in moving from "try" to "do."

Clutter words, such as try, are like balled-up pieces of paper on the floor. They serve no purpose and have no usefulness—plus, you can trip over enough of them. Other clutter words include "maybe," "we'll see what happens," "it depends," and so on. Bottom line: These words can be an excuse. My friend Zolene Bruner says, "Excuse is a dressed-up lie—like a tuxedo is a dressed-up suit."

 **Purpose Point:**
Think of your personal clutter words. Can you remember why you started using them? Make a conscious effort, beginning today, to replace negative words and phrases with positive, life-giving words.

Order Your Mouth

Monitor your mouth. Watch what you say. In one of the Bible studies I teach, I talk about the heart-mind-mouth connection. In Matthew 12:34 (NKJV), Jesus said, "Out of the abundance of the heart, the mouth speaks." In other words, what is in your heart (the seat of your emotions) will make its way to your mind in your thought processes. If your thoughts are negative, they will sprout seeds of worry, fear, and doubt. The next thing you know, you are speaking the negative things you *don't* want to happen out of your own mouth, making them more likely to happen.

 **Purpose Point:**
What negative words are you speaking over your own life?

Order Your Health

Here's the most important reason to consider ordering your health: It is the physical energy resource that helps fuel your future. So many of us are walking around with Big Dreams and no energy to run after them. I was one of those people. My heart's desire was to finish the book you are reading, but my body was too exhausted to sit very long at my computer. Before I could resume this important project, I had to order my health.

See, I'd been plagued with certain health problems nearly since puberty. Not only was I plagued with health problems, I *suffered* with them. Like the woman described in Mark 5, I spent much money, time, and energy working to address the issue. The situation finally reached the point where my illness took over my life. I had done all that I could do. My doctor urged me to schedule major surgery. But two days before I was to enter the hospital, I did some serious praying. At the end of my prayers, I concluded that God did not want me to have the surgery. But to avoid the knife, I had to make some lifestyle changes. The time had come for me to order my health.

When you make the decision to make changes in your life, God will always have someone available to help you get there. My friend Melinda is my health coach. M, as I call her, is a certified nutritional consultant. She addressed her own health issues head-on by going organic. She replaced her sodas and junk food with healthy meals, snacks, and lots of water. She fed nutritious, yummy recipes to her family. Most important, she went deeper in prayer and Bible study, developing an attitude of gratitude. As a result, my five-foot-nothing friend went from a size 12 to a size 2 just by modifying her eating habits. I wouldn't have believed it if I hadn't seen her old photos! Although we had worked at the same company for more than a year, and I was aware of her successes, it wasn't until I was really ready for a change that I reached out to her for help. She created a deceptively simple but powerfully effective plan for me to follow.

Chapter Four — Laying Your Foundation

The results of working "The Plan" that M provided me have been nothing short of amazing. I lost weight, gained energy, and felt well enough to start working out, which increased my fitness and helped me reshape my physique. My skin became clear and luminous. The problems I had struggled with for years miraculously reversed, which was documented by my medical technician. My doctor, who had urged me to schedule surgery, marveled and said, "Whatever you've been doing, keep doing it!"

You know what you need to do. Start with baby steps. Replace your morning lattes with hot tea; at least limit your coffee intake. Sip a glass of lemon water before each meal. Get more rest. Cut out one TV program and get an hour's more sleep. And definitely disconnect from negative people who stress you out! Start small: 50 percent is better than no percent, but 100 percent is better than 75. In other words, you cannot "almost" eat healthy and wonder why you're not getting results. A salad paired with a diet soda is counterproductive.

And you need to be ruthless while you work your plan. Like any other positive steps, when you make a decision to order your health, there are people all too happy to help you fail at your goal. Everybody shows up at the office with some cookies, birthday cake, and fresh-baked brownies. (The co-worker bearing a plate of brownies would be me. I still like to bake.) Last Easter Sunday, I splurged and ate a very small bowl of apple pie and paid for it with health problems for nearly a week.

You don't have to spend hundreds of dollars over your food budget to eat healthier. It may take some planning, but there are ways to buy what you need to help make positive changes in your health.

For example, I live in a major metropolitan area dotted with big-box warehouse clubs. My membership enables me to keep my body fueled properly with fresh, healthy food at reasonable prices. If you have a big family, these clubs are more than worth the annual fee. Even if you don't need to shop there every week, it's always good to have certain staples in stock. Toilet paper, anyone? I shop at the "nothing's over a dollar" stores, too. You'd be surprised at the deals you find there. Scheduling your grocery and other shopping trips helps you order your money.

Some of you will tell yourselves it's too expensive and too much trouble to order your health. I would counter with this one question: *Is it less trouble and expense to end up in the hospital—or the cemetery?*

 **Purpose Point:**
Look in your kitchen pantry right now. Are the foods you are stocking healthy and nutritious? Now look in your refrigerator. Can your body run efficiently on what's inside? Then start throwing it out and replenishing your food supply, one shelf at a time.

Order Your Time

Another good reason for ordering your health is because scheduling your meals helps you *order your time* during the day. Ordering your time keeps you on course for your Big Dream. In chapter 7, we will talk about the Haters, Waiters, and Gators, people who are sent to deter you from your purpose. There are also Drainers, people who steal your time with distractions. It takes a *lot* of focused energy to do your part on the Big Dream. Sadly, many "remora people" are too lazy or fearful to work on ordering their own lives; they steal yours or attach themselves to you to avoid the pain in their own life situations.

The Power of No

(Jesus) saith unto him, Wilt thou be made whole?"
John 5:6 KJV

As a Christian, a minister, and a leader, I reach out to a lot of people. My heart's desire is to help everyone. But I am also learning the power of the word "No." Sometimes people are not ready to receive. Pouring yourself into some people is like pouring water into an upside-down glass. Not everyone wants to be helped.

Sometimes we fill up our lives with our kids, our jobs, or even our church work. All of these are good, but when done out of balance, they can be a feeble attempt to avoid adding order to our worlds. Sometimes you have to step out of other people's lives for a period to step into your purpose and destiny. I'm not saying it's an easy thing to do. I'm a writer, which means I know how to put the "pro" in procrastination! But I am saying, like anything else, each little step will help you get there. Start with saying no to the things that distract you from your Big Dream. Some no's are to people.

 **Purpose Point:**
Stand in front of your mirror. Think of three areas in which you'd like to say no. Practice saying no graciously, but without explanation. "No, I can't. No, I won't be available. No, I'm not interested."

The Power of Yes

We've discussed saying no. Now, what will you say yes to? What will you permit into your thoughts, your speech, and your actions? Remember, there is power in what you say.

Order Your Money

Part of getting our Big Dream done is ordering our money. This is a VERY tough one. A prominent money-management minister says, "Show me your checkbook and I can show you what you value." What do you value? Are you honoring God with your giving? Are you, in my father's words, salting away something in case of an emergency?

Some of you have told me that you can't afford to do your Big Dream. Some of you have told me that it's materialistic to even talk about money. But Jesus Himself did. He answered Peter's plea for tax money. He was concerned about provision. He even provided a post-Resurrection "lunch break" for the disciples. Now, I agree that we live in an era of rampant materialism—within and outside the Church. And I'm writing this book while my country—America—

is in the middle of a very deep, very serious recession. I'm affected by it as well. But I can tell you in all certainty that the church cliché is true: Where God guides, He provides. Every time I have needed something to propel my Big Dream, God has put someone in my path to help me. God is not a spiritual ATM, but He will finance His work. The question is, are you willing to bring order into your life to receive all that He has for you? Are you willing to move where the money is?

I mentioned the big-box warehouse clubs. I live right down the street from one of them. I go there so often they barely ask for my membership card! The annual membership fee is a tool that helps me simultaneously order my time, my money, and my health.

Order Your Surroundings

How do you live? I come from a long line of clutter queens. Organization does not come naturally to me. But as I learn to order my world, I find it easier to master my Y.O.U. The more of my surroundings I keep in order, the better I am able to accomplish my Big Dream. When I look around my home and see things in order, my mind is more tranquil. That helps me to think clear, focused thoughts that flow out of my head through my fingers. I'm learning to make clutter my mortal enemy. Dust bunnies are *not* my friend!

I schedule weekly wash, grocery, and cleaning days. Staying on my routine keeps my world orderly. Whenever I break my focus, the next week's activities get thrown off. Make sense to you?

I'm an avid and voracious reader, but when I'm writing, I intentionally avoid reading a lot (other than the Bible and Internet news sites). I don't want to be overly influenced by other's opinions and positions. One notable exception is a book by an author I've been blessed to meet, Ann Williams Platz of Atlanta. Ann epitomizes Southern grace and charm.

In her 13th book, *Queen Esther's Reflection: A Portrait of Grace, Courage, and Excellence,* Ann uses her formidable powers of influence to retell the story of Queen Esther. In doing so, she coaches women to prepare to meet our destiny. Part of that process includes ordering our surroundings.

I'm ordering my surroundings one room at a time. I'm adding beauty and color to my world. Color affects your mood. Right now, I'm working on my master bedroom. Layered in soothing shades of blue and white, it is looking more and more like a spa retreat. I love it! It's amazing what a difference it makes in my mood when I wake up, before bedtime, and even when I just walk into the room. Make your home a haven. Make time to order your world. Invest in a shredder and, as my friend and assistant, Dawn, urges me, purge, purge, purge.

When I talk about ordering our surroundings, I'm not speaking solely of ordering our homes. I'm talking about our cars, desks, wallets, and purses—whatever we look at, live in or use daily. By the way, ordering your surroundings is not just for women. Men can be notorious for dropping things at the front door and expecting them to miraculously make their way to their proper place.

My next ordering project is my office area. Pray for me . . .

 **Purpose Point:**
Pick a room in your home, any room. Throw away five items right now.

Ordering your Connections

The minister Mike Murdock said, "Loyalty determines access." Jesus Christ used this principle in His ministry. He loved all people; but He had an inner circle, Peter, James, and John, among his 12 disciples. Loyalty determines access. I am a giver and a lover of people. But I have learned to guard what God has placed in my heart by limiting my interactions with people who deter and distract me from my goals. We already discussed attachments vs. connections in Chapter 1. That means my connections have to be ordered to function more effectively. Have you ever been in one airport terminal, headed to another, and missed your connection? That's because timing is everything. Again, be careful not to attach to or connect with people that cause you to miss your destiny connections.

Following a Pattern of Excellence

Many people have a pattern, but not too many people have a pattern of excellence. Can you tell me who the top golfers in the world are? Can you tell me who any of the top ten women tennis players in the world are? Maybe one or two. But everyone knows who Tiger Woods is. Nearly everyone in the world knows who Serena and Venus Williams are. You know who they are because

1) they are blessed with a phenomenal amount of natural talent, and 2) they are disciplined enough to consistently develop and refine that talent. Their worst playing seasons are ones that some of their competitors would dream of. A pattern of excellence is a divinely inspired outline of instruction to achieve a God-honoring result.

Following a pattern of excellence can be boring. It can be dull and tiresome—if you allow it to be. A pattern of excellence comprises the following four elements.

Four factors of a pattern of excellence

1. **High quality of materials.** Have you ever baked a cake with real butter, fresh eggs, real vanilla, rich baking chocolate, real cake flour, fresh ingredients, and a good oven? Now compare it to a microwave cake. It's edible, and it's flavorful, but it just doesn't nourish the soul like something made from scratch. It's not the same effect, is it? The quality of your materials does matter.

2. **High quality of lifestyle.** What would happen if your lifestyle determined whether you could accomplish your Big Dream? Would you be setting yourself up for an epic fail? What steps could you take to improve the way you live your life to get to your Big Dream sooner?

3. **High quality of pattern.** Did you ever attempt to assemble something at home, like a bookcase or an entertainment center, with bad instructions? I write instructions for a living,

and believe me, not much is worse than bad documentation. Is your life blueprint up to code?

4. **High quality of gifts.** I have been blessed with talents, but I didn't always recognize them as such. Many times I would observe others using their gifts, developing their talents, or operating in their circles of influence and think, "If I just had. . . ." Now I realize that God has given each of us what we need to fulfill our purpose and destiny. But it's not enough to simply recognize we have a gift. We have to use it! Practice your craft, your skill, and your passion. He will allow His quality to shine through.

 *Power Point*

Name two things you are REALLY good at, even excellent. Why did you pick those things?

Four hindrances to following a pattern of excellence

1. **The "that'll do" spirit.** This is when things are done according to what's convenient rather than according to what's right. It's the easy way out. Some people breeze through school and obtain a degree, but sadly, they fail to get an education. The detail is in the application. I had a friend who was getting married. She was paying great attention to every detail of the wedding and was sharing it with me, her maid of honor. The time came to discuss the cake. Being raised with my mother's elegant taste, I was thinking of one

of the two finer bakeries in our city. She said, "I'm thinking of getting it at (a local supermarket)." I was shocked. She got mad and threatened to leave. Hey, don't hate me because I prefer excellence if I can get it.

2. **The "Lone Ranger" spirit.** Your Big Dream will take you *and* your Building Crew to accomplish it. You absolutely cannot do it alone.

3. **The "Who do you think you are?" spirit.** This is when you question yourself or let other people disqualify you for your Big Dream. Someone's going to do it—why *not* you?

4. **The "somebody (else) ought to do something" spirit.** That's when you're waiting for someone else to do what *you* see needs doing.

What's in Your Hand?

To the people protesting, saying they don't have what it takes, I respond, "What's in your hand?" God is not concerned with what you have to start with; He's moved by your actions based on faith. He is faithful in giving you what you need as you use what you have. As I have used my talents to bless others, God has opened doors of opportunity for me to be blessed and be a blessing. What do you do that you enjoy doing? What's special about you? What do you bring to the table of life that is unique? What do you have at your disposal right now? Don't worry about the ending—just use what you have to get started!

We've done some foundational work here. In the next chapter, we are going to begin building. This is not a cakewalk process. It is not easy. If it were easy, anybody could do it. But *you* can! Roll up your sleeves and let's get started. Are you ready?

Five Steps to a New Y.O.U.

1. Ask for God's best.

2. Believe for God's best.

3. Work for God's best.

4. Look for God's best.

5. Do *your* best.

A Prayer for You

Father, as we lay our foundation, we want to thank You for the progress made so far. We ask Your divine help as we do the hard work to add order to our lives. Help us to walk in a spirit of excellence, and we celebrate even the baby steps of success. In Your Son's name, Amen.

Reflective Questions

- Have you started excavating your life?
- Are you following a pattern of excellence?
- What relationship connections do you need to reorder?
- What do you have in your hand right now to get started with?
- What preparation steps can you start making right now?

Building Your House

Chapter 5

If GOD doesn't build the house, the builders only build shacks. Psalm 127:1 (MSG)

Jesus was not the only carpenter in biblical times. It was a major occupation for many reasons. For one thing, people were generally more nomadic. They were also more exposed to natural disasters, so something always had to be built or rebuilt. As a result of the times they lived in, Jesus used many examples, parables, and stories related to building.

What does it take to build? Proverbs 24:3-4 (NIV) tells us the key components:

*By wisdom a house is built,
 and through understanding it is established;*

*Through knowledge its rooms are filled
 with rare and beautiful treasures.*

Here are three key components to work with:

1. Wisdom

2. Understanding

3. Knowledge

Let's start with number three and work our way up: Knowledge knows *what* to do; understanding knows *how* to do; and wisdom knows *why*, *when*, and *where*.

With apologies to the architect and builders who may be reading this book, I compare the building process to three general levels of construction:

1. The foundation

2. The frame

3. The façade

The Foundation
When a building project first begins, the only thing you see for quite a while is one big hole in the ground. Doesn't look like much at first, does it? But eventually, the cement trucks start backing up to the lot, and dirt starts flying. Having worked for some time as a professional writer, I've noted that most clients want to see dirt flying (uploaded, printed or PDF pages) before the foundation is dug (proper research is completed). I'm told that the normal home foundation is about three inches thick. One particular man was the contractor of his own home, and he built his house on a six-inch

slab—just in case. Take the time to build properly. You may have to dig deeper, and the process may take longer, but the ultimate product—your Big Dream—will be stronger.

The Frame

Once the foundation is poured, the walls begin to go up. When you drive by a house in this stage, you can identify whether it's one story or two, where the windows are, where the plumbing will be placed, which way it will face. As your Big Dream forms, at the frame stage you can start to have an idea of what it might look like. But remember, God is the ultimate Architect. He has the final sign-off on the finished work.

The Façade

Finally, this is where the building begins to take shape. The brick is selected; the windows and shutters are installed . . . that's when it "looks" like a house! But really, it was a house as soon as someone drove by an area, purchased acreage, and said, that's where I'm going to start building!

It's funny, but at the façade stage, the general public usually begins to take interest in a Big Dream; whether it is a business, a building, a church, or even a person. I've heard many stories about people who gave up on a project *or an individual* while in their foundation stage only to find the next person grab it, take it to façade stage, and enjoy the benefits of someone else's work.

> *Though your beginning was insignificant,*
> *Yet your end will increase greatly.* Job 8: (NASB)

Take the time to build something of lasting value. We live in a celebrity culture, where people are famous for being famous, famous for being infamous, and famous for being scandalous. There are even people who are famous for simply knowing someone famous. That is a false façade. Having a beautiful outside is nothing if there is no depth behind it. Don't despise your foundation stage. The end result will be well worth it.

Seven Steps to Building a Strong House

1. Take your vision to God.

2. Get ready (prepare) to build.

3. Write down your Big Dream (vision).

4. Share it with your Building Crew.

5. Count the cost for the house.

6. Gather your materials for the house.

7. Beware of distractions and detractors.

The Building Crew

Just as iron sharpens iron, friends sharpen the minds of each other.   Proverbs 27:17 (CEV)

When I was a little girl, I played with Lego, those small, colorful plastic bricks that connect together to build things. The name

Lego comes from the Danish "leg godt," which means to "play well." I believe that play is an essential ingredient in a child's development. It grows the human spirit. Playing encourages imagination, conceptual thinking, creation, and teamwork. Lego is a wonderful toy. I loved building things with it. But what can you build, ultimately, with just one Lego? Building your Big Dream is like building a wonderful skyscraper. To build great things, you need a Building Crew.

When you pursue your Big Dream, it's critical that you surround yourself with the right people to build the right structure. Otherwise, you can set out to build a skyscraper and end up building a shack. I'm not talking about an entourage, or a posse, or a bunch of folks who just like being around you. Nor am I speaking of your family members, though your Crew may include them. I'm speaking of a God-connection of people who come together to accomplish a Big Dream.

Your Building Crew must have several qualifications:

- Each person must be spiritually, emotionally, and financially balanced in his or her own life (or committed to actively working toward being so).
- Each person must absolutely care about you as a person.
- Each person must be absolutely committed to your success.
- Each member must be able to "play well with others."
- Each member must bring something to the table that you can learn and benefit from.
- Each member must be able to speak freely into your life — whether you are right *or* wrong.

My Crew meets and exceeds those qualifications. It's important to set those parameters because you need at least a baseline balance for a successful Big Dream. I'm not talking about the people who call you periodically and tell you they are praying for you, although those are important to have. I'm talking about people who are "ride or die," who are invested in seeing you get there. Those people are extremely hard to find; they should be treasured like diamonds when you do.

Here's another important qualification: *You* must be able to bring something to the table that benefits your team. This should be a win-win situation. Although you are working to achieve your Big Dream, this is not about what you can *get from* people. It's about what you can *bring to* people.

I can't say this enough: Your purpose and destiny can be furthered *or* hindered by your connection to another person or persons. That's why the people you connect with are very important. Choose wisely.

Purpose Point:
Write down five people whom you believe are qualified candidates for your Building Crew. Why did you select them?

Naomis and Mordecais

All leaders (and by that I mean us) need mentors in their lives, mature people with the wealth of understanding and the wisdom of time and perspective.

I have been privileged to make the acquaintances of many "Naomis" and "Mordecais," named after the biblical mentors. Each woman has wells of wisdom and knowledge that I have been blessed to draw from. I also have a close circle of father and brother figures in my life that I can call on if needed for guidance. There are so many other women and men, from my own mother and father to other relatives and friends, who are dear to my heart.

Ruths and Joshuas

I have younger friends, "Ruths" and "Joshuas." Later in his life, the jazz legend Miles Davis surrounded himself with "young guns," musicians with their own viewpoints and styles whom the legend could learn from and teach. The multitalented musician Prince does the same thing. The graphic and Web designers I have worked with (usually younger) have taught me so much about how to use the power of technology to share my message. I value their talent, their creativity, and their ability to teach me new things.

Younger adults also help inoculate your spirit against older people who are always looking for the reason something can't be done. Younger people are usually brimming with enthusiasm and a positive attitude. I like being around them. To be clear: I don't try to be 25; not that I ever could. I just ask questions, listen, and learn while simultaneously balancing their exuberance with my own wisdom. Many of my younger friends have brought both preternatural wisdom and practical information. I get to teach them some things as well. It's a win-win all the way around.

As You Build

- Write your vision.
- Share your vision with your Building Crew.
- Watch out for detractors and distractions (chapter 7)
- Celebrate your progress.
- Run to win!

You know that many runners enter a race, and only one of them wins the prize. So run to win!
                                   1 Corinthians 9:24 (CEV)

 **Power Point:**
Name three things that you have accomplished since you started pursuing your Big Dream. Celebrate how these accomplishments have improved your life.

A Prayer for You

Father, we thank You for the courage to build our Big Dreams. Let us "play well" with others as we watch it take shape. We celebrate our Ruths, Mordecais, Naomis and Joshuas who accompany us. We take time to appreciate our Building Crew. Most of all, we do not despise our small beginnings. In Your Son's Name, Amen.

Reflective Questions

- What are the foundation, the frame, and the façade of your house?
- Have you assembled your Building Crew yet?
- Who are the Ruths, Joshuas, Naomis, and Mordecais in your life?

CHAPTER SIX — FURNISHING AND DECORATING

Furnishing and Decorating

Chapter 6

Faith by itself, if it is not accompanied by action, is dead.
James 2:17

Life is characterized by movement. From a newborn's first gasping gulp of air to a dying man's last ragged exhale, movement is an extension of the life that we lead. We even make nouns into verbs to express the movement of our lives: We "party;" we "message" our friends and colleagues; we "punk" our friends when playing a practical joke. We've even hijacked the vocal stylings of birds to convey quick communication: We *tweet*.

Most activities are even less fun if we're not moving while doing them. Would you rather watch a football game or an opera?

God Himself is the progenitor, or the originator, of movement. In Genesis 1, the Spirit of God moved over the face of the waters. That word for move, *rachaph*, means to brood, or to move in a relaxed manner. In other words, the Spirit of the Creator was waiting to be called to attention by the Creator.

Living things that don't eventually move are generally considered stagnant and eventually defined as dead. Stagnant water is not considered fit to drink. Stagnant air is foul and stale. People who don't have the ability to move under their own power have to be turned in their beds to avoid bedsores. Even bears only hibernate for a season. God expects His creatures to move! Movement indicates life, activity, and purpose. Those of us who have been preserved for a purpose understand that it isn't enough just to have a Big Dream. You've got to move toward making your Big Dream happen.

Waiting to Exhale—or Waiting to Expire?

The Hebrew word for breath is *ruach*. Hospitals use the term "expire" when they are telling you a patient just passed away. I have watched a person being born, and I have watched a person die. There is nothing more agonizing than waiting for that first or last breath.

In Genesis 2:7, where God breathed life into man, the Hebrew word used to describe it was *nesh-aw-maw*, which can mean "divine inspiration." God divinely inspired man at his "birth," and hard-coded purpose and destiny in him. In Genesis 2:8 God put the man in the garden and told him to go to work! That word *soom* means "to appoint, to ordain, to put in order." I believe in training and preparation, but I never read in Genesis that God put man on probation or in a training program.

Make Your Move

> *And he said unto them, How is it that ye sought me? wist ye not that I must be about my Father's business?*
> Luke 2:49 (KJV)

After you have done your excavation and laid your foundation, it's now time to be about the business of building your Big Dream. When it comes to my Big Dream, I must confide to you that I'm of the "it's better to ask forgiveness than permission" school of thought. I'd rather be redirected by God while I am making my move, than wait for permission to move from someone who doesn't have an interest or concern in my Big Dream anyway. Now, just in case you think I'm a loose cannon, I didn't say Big Dreamers don't need education, discipline, or mentoring. These are critical. I have a college education with plans to go further. I carefully, prayerfully weigh options before I make a move. I also have spiritual, business, creative, technical, and financial mentors who walk in integrity and speak words of caution and insight into my decision-making process. But in terms of my purpose, there are some things inside of me that *I just know*. Some things, like your Big Dreams, don't have gatekeepers. You may not be "there" yet: You may need a mentor, you may need training, and you may need someone to help unlock your purpose. You may need someone to help encourage you and build you up and prepare you to receive it. You will need others to tell people about you. You may even occasionally need someone to keep you from talking yourself out of it—but *it* is inside you! What are you waiting for? Don't talk about it—*be* about it!

You're Burning Daylight

Sometimes, we are waiting for something to happen when "it" has already happened. Stop and take a deep breath right now. Are you breathing? OK, you have been appointed and preserved for something. Too often, we are waiting for permission when He already gave us permission to live. In John 10:10, Jesus said that He "came that we might have life, and have it abundantly (NASB)." That word for life, *zoe*, means more than salvation. It indicates wholeness and balance—to possess life to the max. But we must be careful not to waste our most precious resource—our time. Back at the ranch of life, in the words of my late father, we are "burning daylight." We are waiting to exhale, not realizing that we are really waiting to expire. The first part of John 10:10 reads that the thief comes to steal, kill, and destroy. While you're waiting for your turn to live, you are also waiting your turn to die. You're burning daylight—make your move!

What's Your Focus?

Power is nothing without focus. I sometimes watch hunting programs. I don't know whether I have the stomach to hunt, but I respect the sport. I see the hunters watch the animal make its way to the clearing, carefully set the goal within their site scope, wait till the right moment, and then pull the trigger. The aftermath is just as precise. First the field dressing, then the cleaning, the cutting, and the other tasks that go along with preparing the kill for dinner or taxidermy. All that focus for a target that either gets eaten or hung on a wall. Targets require focus.

Chapter Six — Furnishing and Decorating

One of the definitions of focus is "the point at which rays of light, heat, or other radiation meet after being refracted or reflected." Sometimes, you just need a little illumination. Other times, you need a fire lit under you to get going! Truth be told, some of us wouldn't take the first step toward our goals if we didn't have a little heat under us. Set your focus on your Big Dream.

What's Your Target?

Focus is nothing without a target. And I'm not talking about the store. A target is "an object, usually marked with concentric circles, to be aimed at in shooting practice or contests." Those concentric red-and-white circles help you define what you are after. While working toward your Big Dream, think about the *why* as well as the *what* of your goals.

What's Your Purpose?

A target is nothing without a purpose for hitting the target. Have you ever reached a goal and wondered, *Is that all there is?* Perhaps you had no purpose in mind for the goals you had set. Sometimes people do something without thinking about the reason they are doing them. I used to frequent a wonderful restaurant when I lived in another city. They had the best fresh-fruit pancakes in town. My favorite waiter was a guy named Steve. Steve was lively, funny, always pleasant, and scarily insightful (he was able to correctly tell *you* what you wanted for breakfast!). Steve was also the most overqualified waiter I ever met. He had two master's degrees and was working on a third when I moved out of the city. And his majors weren't something simple; no, they were extremely technical. Steve had the power. He certainly had the focus. He hit his targets with ease. But he seemingly had no purpose for achieving his goals.

 **Purpose Point:**
List five steps that you have taken toward pursuing your Big Dream.

What Are Your Motives?

What's your motive for achieving your Big Dream? Your motives must be pure as well. "I want to make a billion dollars so I can live next door to Jay-Z and Beyonce" isn't gonna cut it. Pure motives ensure that you not only become blessed, but also become a blessing yourself.

What's the Result?

Achieving your goal is nothing without results that measure against expectations. In other words, don't stop until the job is done according to plan. Have you ever ordered something that wasn't what you expected once you received it? Say I promised you a new Porsche on a certain date. On the special day, if I showed up with a toy model car, wouldn't you be disappointed? Then you have an idea of what I mean by measurable results.

Power + Focus + Target + Purpose + Measurable Results = Strategy

Put all these elements together and you have a Divine Strategy to accomplish your Big Dream and the Directive Destiny for your life!

Are We There Yet?

When you were a little kid, did you ever go on a road trip and nag your parents with the dreaded words, "Are we there yet?" That's because even in your childlike mind, you understood that a goal is nothing without measurable results.

Although you shouldn't stop until the job is done according to plan, don't forget to enjoy the view along the way. The unexpected surprise in pursuing your Big Dream is how it changes you for the better. Sometimes your Big Dream doesn't look exactly like you thought it would. But if you stay focused on God, it will be perfect for you.

Become a Five-Talent Steward

There's a story in Matthew 25 about three servants, or stewards. Each of them had been given a certain number of "talents" by his master. They were left with the instructions to invest, or multiply, those talents. One steward was given five talents; the second, three. The third steward was given only one.

The first two put their talents to work. The third took his one single talent and hid it in the ground. When the master returned, the servant had the nerve to blame the master for his own laziness and inactivity. Notice two things: 1) The master did not put any requirements on the results; 2) the master took the one buried talent and gave it to the ones who worked with what they had. Our Master rewards according to faithfulness, not amount of talent.

The moral of this story is, work what you've got! Don't sit on your gift. If your one talent is baking chocolate chip cookies, bake every chance you get. If it's an encouraging word, stop, put this book down, and give the gift of encouragement to someone. If it's sending up a silent prayer for someone you pass by in the supermarket, say it. Work it! Work your gift. God is watching to see what you will do with what He has given you. You have been through too much hell to sit on your gift. Someone needs what you have. Stop worrying about the outcome of your actions. Stop wondering who is watching you (or not) or whether someone will come alongside you to help you. Do *your* part. You work your gift and watch God go to work for you. Work it!

You think you have only one talent? Then work the one single talent you have, and watch it multiply! If you don't do something with what has been given you, don't blame someone else for your lack of success. If you don't work your gift and others around you do, don't look hatefully at their blessings and successes. They did the work to get where they are. They endured the pain, they worked their gift, and they get to enjoy the fruit of their labor.

It's a sad thing to sit on your gifting. So many people wait for someone to give them permission to live. While you are waiting for them, God is waiting for you!

 **Purpose Point:**
Identify *one* talent you would gladly do for the rest of your life if you could. Take a step toward working that talent today!

The Price of Persistence

. . . is pain. There's no getting around it: There. Will. Be. Pain. Your Big Dream will hurt. Pain will sometimes, often come in the form of having to be the *only* one who encourages you. (That's why they call it *self*-esteem.) At other times, it's the crush of loneliness and the chill of rejection from people who haven't seen the dirt flying yet. I trained for a marathon briefly, and I was told that in training, you never run a full marathon until the day of the race. You are in the middle of the race. Don't stop now. The price of persistence is *pain*. It's living with loneliness and rejection while your entire being cries out for your Big Dream to be celebrated. It's deferring the feeling of accomplishment and the psychic sigh of completion to struggle through the frustration of fortitude.

Let go of the way it *is* to have it the way you want it. Let go of waiting for a safety zone—emotional, financial, social or otherwise—before you fully focus on your Big Dream. Let go of the childlike training-wheel fantasy of having lots of people run alongside, encouraging and supporting you every step of the way. The price of persistence is pain. It's ignoring the real human desire for the warmth of validation and the aural massage of applause. Persist—whether you receive encouragement or not.

So what if someone thinks you are spinning your wheels? Some may think you have no wheels at all! Some will forever see you as parked on the side of the road, or on cinder blocks in the front yard of life. But only you know—no, wait a minute, maybe you don't—how close you are to your Big Dream.

Beware of people who try to convince you that your pain is permanent, that mediocrity is to be expected. We didn't experience our own versions of Dante's rings of hell to live a life of complacency. We were not created to be walking around resigned to less than our purpose and potential.

Pain has power. Paying the price of persistence is, my friend, what makes you *you*. Pain is the currency of authenticity and of excellence. Pain puts a stamp on you that no one can imitate or duplicate. Pain ensures that anyone who tries to mimic or hurt you will not come even close to succeeding because they haven't gone through what you went through to get there. Authenticity makes the difference between lightning and a lightning bug.

Pain is a valuable tool in accomplishing your Big Dream. Pain reminds you not to revisit your past. Pain is an indicator of growth: It informs you that your muscles are stretching. Pain proves that you are getting stronger. Pain indicates that you are alive. Adam and Eve, when evicted from the Garden of Eden, were kept from returning to their place of punishment by two angels posted at the entrance, hoisting flaming swords. Sometimes, when I'm tempted to go back to places in my past, I remind myself of the pain I experienced. I imagine those two angels posted at the entrance to my past. Then I think of what my Big Dream looks like, what it feels and sounds and smells like. It makes my present pain less problematic. Make your pain work for you.

Chapter Six — Furnishing and Decorating

Patience for the Promise

> *And the LORD visited Sarah as he had said, and the LORD did unto Sarah as he had spoken.*   Genesis 21:1 (KJV)

Sarah, the "mother" of the Hebrew nation, was in a situation. Her name meant "princess," but when she is introduced to us in Genesis 11:29-30, she is instantly defined by what she *didn't* have. "Sarah was barren." She married Abram (later called Abraham), who was an extremely wealthy older man. Still beautiful in advanced age, she obediently followed her husband from the familiarity of the country called Ur into an unknown future. Her stigma followed her.

In Near Eastern culture, barrenness was considered a curse brought on by some unconfirmed sin, so she was likely relegated to the sidelines of the women's subculture. Perhaps Sarah was relied upon to do the babysitting chores for the young mothers. Maybe she was shunned by the usual clique who gathered by the stream during the day to do laundry and gossip. You see, to associate with a woman like Sarah was to associate with one of life's losers. Yet this woman was God's chosen woman of promise.

I believe I have some personal insight into how Sarah must have felt. At this stage in my life, I have never been married, and I have no children. There are things that God has promised me, both in my ministry and in my personal life, that have not yet come to pass. I've moved past the stage where I bump into old classmates, colleagues, and acquaintances who query, "So, when are you getting married?" Instead they ask, "You never did get married, did you?" It's easy to start feeling like expired meat—like those single sitcom characters who are always popping up in their married friends' kitchens. I've felt left out in social settings because most other women my age are talking about the latest happenings of their husbands or children. Some are talking about their grandchildren. I generally talk about current affairs, techno-gadgets, family, ministry, my writing career, their lives—or my cat.

I know what it's like to feel like the fifth wheel in a society where—and I'm talking about Christianity, the Church at large here—God's paradigm, one of his His perfect expressions of His love for us, is the family. And at this writing, I don't have one of my own. In the Church, the family of God, engagements, marriages, and babies are celebrated, and singleness is often ignored or even held suspect. In some cases, singles are exploited for their availability, flexibility, discretionary income, overeagerness to serve, and other characteristics.

To be clear, I'm not sitting around wearing a pair of fuzzy slippers and a bathrobe, eating a pint of premium ice cream, and feeling sorry for myself. I've got too much to do! But I have experienced the pain of rejection because I didn't fit in. I understand all too well what it feels like to be disqualified by my past, to be rejected by the "mean girl" clique, to be scorned by church folk. I've been too young, too old, too smart, not technical enough, too religious, too ethnic, not ethnic enough—you name it. So, I can imagine how Sarah must have felt in a culture that marked her as imperfect, unimportant, and insignificant for the one thing she was unable to change about herself. Then she tried taking matters into her own hands, with disastrous results. After that fiasco, Sarah had little choice but to wait for God to produce what He had promised and what only He could provide.

During the course of her marriage to Abraham, Sarah experienced deceit, disappointment, derision, and despair. Her husband, whom she had known since childhood, and whom she had faithfully followed to Canaan, had betrayed her twice. Yet this was God's woman of promise.

Sarah was not perfect in her patience. She gave her own husband permission to sleep with another woman to bear a child she could raise as her own. How desperate is that? We can scorn Sarah when we read her story from a historical distance, but I confess that I, too, haven't been perfect in my patience. Hardly anyone is. Sometimes desperate situations lead people to do desperate things.

Sarah was defined by her societal situation. Yet God promised her that she would be the mother of a nation. Her current definition was not her ultimate destiny. Are you defined by your situation? Do people know what you did, even define you for it but don't know who you are?

Sarah didn't go crazy. When the time came, she went to the tent and went to work. Operate out of your strengths, not your weaknesses.

 **Purpose Point:**
Make a decision right now to stop defining yourself by your faults, shortcomings, and flaws. Select three things about *you* to celebrate today.

Prerequisites for the Promise

    Prayer

    Patience

    Preparation

    Persistence

What's in a Name?

I'm telling you that God will change your name before He can change your circumstances. I don't mean that literally. I am referring to lining up what God's Word says about you with what *you* think about you. You have to realize that whatever you thought of yourself, the only opinion that matters is God's. My mother told me a story about my childhood. She said I ran up to her at our outdoor clothesline asking, "Mommy, are we rich?" Being well aware of the humble neighborhood we lived in, my mother wondered why I was asking. I exclaimed, "Because Daddy says we're rich!"

It doesn't matter what your circumstances look like. It doesn't matter what other people say about you. The only opinion that really matters is Daddy's.

Open House

One of the exciting things about building a house is bringing your friends over to see your dream come true. But you wouldn't put a notice on Facebook inviting everyone within a five-mile radius to stop by! Make sure you don't invite everyone to the Open House of your Big Dream, as we'll discuss in Chapter 7.

Remember:

> Every promise has pitfalls.
>
> Every promise has processes.
>
> Every process has problems.
>
> Every problem has a purpose.
>
> Every purpose has the opportunity for power and peace.

Our purposes have pitfalls, but you can have the opportunity for peace in the middle of your process.

A Prayer for You

Father, thank you for the progress we've made so far. Thank you for spurring us into action. Help us to deal with detractors and focus on the finish lines in our lives. In Your Son's name, Amen.

Reflective Questions

- What are you waiting for to get moving on your Big Dream?

- What promises are you waiting for?

- What "name" have you given yourself? What name have others given you? How have these names affected your life?

- Are you working your talent(s)?

- Who are you planning to invite to your Open House? Who are you disinviting?

Chapter Seven — Scar Stories and Star Stories

Scar Stories and Star Stories

Then (Jesus) said to Thomas, "Reach your finger here, and look at My hands; and reach your hand here, and put it into My side. Do not be unbelieving, but believing." And Thomas answered and said to Him, "My Lord and my God."
John 20:27-29 NKJV

Chapter 7

Like most people my age, I have a few scars on my body. I have some scars from everyday bumps and bruises, and I have some scars from surgery. There is one scar in particular that I rarely think about. I had a large, egg-shaped polyp on my shoulder. It wasn't painful as much as it was noticeable. When people saw me, they thought I was wearing one shoulder pad!

One pastor tried to pray it away. It didn't help. I tried to ignore it. That didn't help either. Finally, I decided to seek medical attention. The doctor who removed the polyp was a skilled plastic surgeon. After my surgery, the doctor proudly brought me proof of his work: the offending tissue in a glass flask. Using formidable precision, he reattached the skin in such a way that unless you looked closely, you wouldn't notice that I had something wrong with me. All that is left is a very thin scar.

There are some injuries, heart scars I call them, in our lives that are noticeable. They weren't prayed away. They couldn't be ignored. But God, the Master Surgeon, can separate us from the source of our pain in a way that only He can do. The events still happened. The past still occurred. Sometimes we see evidence of what He removed. But the pain is gone. All that is left is a scar to remind you where you came from.

The Old Testament patriarch Jacob had a divine encounter with God. He literally wrestled with an angel. His wrestling forced the hand of the angel. He told the angel, "I will not let you go until you bless me." The angel granted his wish but touched him in the hollow of his thigh. Jacob was left with a limp, but he limped away with a blessing! We may have been hurt by life; we may even be scarred a few times. But there is a blessing that comes from hanging on to God in the tough times.

Incremental Greatness

Sometimes we become discouraged while pursuing our Big Dream because we are looking for the "big win." We keep throwing the life equivalent of a Hail Mary pass. Although those do happen, they happen rarely. We wind up ignoring life's little victories. Those are the ones that really count.

NFL Hall of Famer Emmitt Smith didn't become the NFL leading rusher of all time with big yardage. His solid, stocky body, which caused him to be overlooked by coaches and critics alike, uniquely designed him to do what he did successfully for so many seasons. Sometimes the thing that causes others to pass you over is the one thing that propels you into your destiny. See, Emmitt Smith was not a flashy runner. He was not known for the dazzling big plays. But he was effective. He achieved greatness one yard at a time.

Greatness, you see, is not measured by the big accomplishments. Greatness is not measured by financial wealth, by notoriety, by power or influence. Rather, greatness is measured in increments. It is measured by the small moments of love you share on a daily basis. It is measured by the sacrificial gesture. It is measured by how your time is prioritized. It is measured, most of all, by the imprint of your name upon another's heart.

Haters, Waiters, and Gators

> *Do not be misled: "Bad company corrupts good character."*
> 1 Corinthians 15:33 (NIV)

If you haven't realized it by this point, recognize it now: No Big Dream goes unopposed. There will always be people who don't like what you are attempting to do. Hear me clearly: *Don't expect everyone to celebrate you.* Not everyone is happy that you want a better life. What if you succeed more than they? What if you mature, outgrow them and leave their group? Why should you be entitled to success? Besides, you've gotten accustomed to mediocrity and misery; why change now? Every person who is truly committed to change will have a critic. Or two. Or three. Or ten.

I think there are three main categories of critics: I call them the Haters, the Waiters, and the Gators. The Haters are well documented. They are the people who appear out of the woodwork as soon as you announce your Big Dream. They are the ones who remind you of all the failed diets, the wasted money, the thwarted attempts. I have a young friend who not long ago announced her plans to have gastric bypass surgery. As soon as she did, some of her own relatives told her she was lazy and crazy for doing so. Against their opposition, she had the surgery. At this writing, she has lost 140 pounds! She made her decision, feels and looks fantastic, and is experiencing a better life. Some people prefer you to be miserable with them than be happy somewhere else.

The Haters are the ones who despise you for daring to dream the Big Dream, for folding the dream into a vision, for mapping out a strategy to achieve it and sticking to the plan no matter how difficult it gets. Haters also show up *after* you accomplish your Big Dream. They can always find something wrong with what you did.

Here's one way to deal with the Haters: Ignore them. Two men in the Bible were critics of a man named Nehemiah, who was building a great wall for God and His people. One of the men, under the pretense of wanting a friendly dialog, asked Nehemiah to come down from the wall to explain his vision to them. Their ulterior motive was murder. Nehemiah wisely refused the request. Not everyone who smiles in your face is your friend.

The best way to address the Haters is to shine. Focus on your future, not your foes. Some people feed on your adversity like moviegoers with a tub of buttered popcorn. Starve them. You are on your way to becoming a game changer; you don't have time to deal with people who want you on the bench. Nothing succeeds like success.

Too many people want you to waste time explaining your vision to them. You can miss your window of success trying to explain what is in your heart to Haters, who usually don't really care anyway. They just want to murder your Big Dream. Ignore them. Shine around them. And prayerfully avoid them.

The Waiters are more subtle. They don't necessary adopt a public opinion. They wait and see how things turn out in your life. If you do well, they say, "Great! I knew she could do it!" but if you fail . . . "Well, I never expected him to accomplish much anyway." Sometimes, Waiters come in the form of people who want to hang out with you to waste your time while you are working. Whether they intend to or not, they can be a drain on your time, energy, and emotions.

Address the Waiters in much the same way: with silence and disinformation. Don't talk so much. Seal the leaks in your life. Don't waste time trying to explain your efforts. In the movie White Men Can't Jump, one character said that some people would rather look good and lose than look bad and win. Don't be afraid to look bad. Let people assume your smile hides stupidity. Let them wonder. It's OK if they think it's not going well. The Waiters will know the truth soon enough.

The Gators are similar to the Waiters, but when your job/ministry/business/recovery has barely started, they want to kill it, own it, or distract you from nurturing it. I get the name Gators from the alligators who watch turtles lay their eggs in the sand. Once the egg has been laid, the alligator stealthily makes his way to the sand, digs the egg up, and feasts on something someone else has labored to give birth to.

Like their namesake, Gators function this way largely because it's easier to feed off someone else's resources than to develop their own. Sometimes Gators don't have the desire or ability to start something themselves. Perhaps they don't think *you* have the right to achieve your vision without their input (in other words, telling you what they think it should look like). They usually don't want to help you while you're working but want to move into your structure once it is built.

There's a book I read during my childhood called *The Little Red Hen*. The hen wanted to bake a loaf of bread. But when she asked for help planting the wheat for the bread, none of the other animals would come to her aid. The harvesting and baking process got the same negative response. But when the aroma of freshly baked bread came wafting through the barnyard, everyone came running.

The Gators are like that. That's why I told you it's important to have your Building Crew around you early in your process, no matter how small the Crew is to begin with. That way, you're less tempted to talk to the wrong people in hopes of gaining support.

Confront the Gators. Put them in check. Like a mama bear guarding her cubs, you have to be passionate about guarding your Big Dream. What God has for you is for *you*. Do not give it away. I understand that God will protect us. But we have to be careful to guard what He has given us. Guard your hearts.

Beware of people who act as if they believe that for them to be big, you have to be small. Personally, I've fought too hard to be *me*. I have no interest in giving that up. I'm not talking about being honorable or submissive when appropriate, or not respecting other's opinions. I'm talking about working overtime to please other people so much that you don't even know who *you* are anymore.

During a memorable ministry conference a few years ago, I enjoyed a delicious seafood lunch with some pastors. They enthusiastically "got it" when I shared my new ministry vision. The lunch ended with encouragement and prayer for my success. On the way home, I thanked God in prayer for the meeting. He spoke to me, "Do you feel important?" I answered carefully, "No, I feel validated." He responded, "*I* validated you." Point taken. God wants you to get your cues from Him. When you pursue your Big Dream, you will likely have Haters, Waiters, and Gators in your life. But you will be less influenced by them and more affected by *Him*.

I have wasted so much time waiting for the Haters, Waiters, and Gators to "bless" my efforts. But while I was waiting for them, God was waiting for *me*! I went from here to there, listening to offers of help, blessing, and covering that never seemed to pan out. All the while God was directing my path and providing me with what I needed when I needed it. Now, my nomadic journey was not wasted at all. God's leading was strategic. He blessed me to be exposed to and participate in various ministry styles and cultures. He also used me to bring diversity, and with the gifts he placed in me, to be a blessing to other churches. I made connections and formed relationships that forever changed my life for the better.

> *You prepare a table before me in the presence of my enemies.*
> Psalm 23:5 (NIV)

The Haters, Waiters, and Gators will never completely leave your life. But like using a good room freshener, you can neutralize their influence by dispersing "positive ions" of praise, prayer, and worship. It's not that the "stink" doesn't exist; it just loses its potency in the air. When you focus on what is positive in your life, HWGs lose their power. When the Haters, Waiters, and Gators cannot get a knee-jerk reaction from you with their comments; when you stop allowing yourself to be affected by their toxic behavior; when you start responding instead of reacting, even if they still exist in your life, HWGs will lose their influence over you. Your life will become more of a drama-free zone.

HWG Sandwich

One more thing: When you start to realize your Big Dream, expect Haters, Waiters, and Gators at the next level too. That's because some people at that level are not happy about you making it there. They don't realize that there is more than enough abundance to go around. Some next-level Waiters will watch you scrap, save, and strive as you achieve your Big Dream. Then they may be willing to help you, because they were waiting to see what *you* did before they reached out. They offer a leg up, not a bailout. We already know what the Gators do. So don't worry about the HWG sandwich. God's got your back.

 **Purpose Point:**
List three Haters, Waiters, and Gators in your life. Think of three ways you can neutralize their influence on you.

The Wall

One of the goals on my bucket list is to run a marathon. I'm told that when running, you will eventually hit a Wall. That's the point when your knees get wobbly, your legs turn to rubber, and your mouth turns to ashes. Your lungs feel like they are about to explode. Every fiber in your being is telling you to give up. The Wall doesn't happen at the beginning of the race. Not in the middle either. The Wall happens just before the finish line.

There is a point in the pursuit of our Big Dreams when we feel we absolutely cannot go on. It happens to nearly every one of us. It feels like everything is coming apart. That does not mean that the Big Dream was not real or valid. It means that it's time for you to follow the instructions found in 1 Peter 5:6-7 (NKJV): "Humble yourselves therefore under the mighty hand of God, that He may exalt you in due time. Casting all your care upon Him, for he cares for you." When you humble yourself to God, bringing Him your fears, hurts, and concerns, you put yourself in a position for Him to move supernaturally.

Let me tell you a secret: The Wall usually happens right before your Big Dream breaks through. Then God may give you a second wind to complete your run. Remember, it's not how you start—it's how you finish.

God will break you through your Wall if you press in.

The Rest Stop

We all get tired. It's not surprising; it's expected even. Pursuit of your Big Dream can and will wear you down mentally and physically. Pain can be an indicator of fatigue. Physically, pain helps you to realize that something in your life is not working. It may be time for a quick break in the action.

It's OK at times to rest. Find a safe place to nurture your body and your spirit. By now, you should have made your home your haven. Go to your Rest Stop and take care of *you*. Keep healthy foods in stock for the times of fatigue and exhaustion. This is no time to overload on the carbs, the sugar, and the caffeine. Of course, I personally think dark chocolate is OK. . . .

Have an alternative Rest Stop outside your home (one that is Hater, Waiter, and Gator free). Maybe it's a good friend's house or your favorite Starbucks during their downtime. Ask someone on your Building Crew if you can stop by occasionally and grab a sandwich, rest, and get some encouragement.

But don't lose heart if you can't find a Rest Stop. Sometimes you can't find a friend. But you can always find a friend in God. At one point in his reign, even King David had to encourage *himself* when his entire army abandoned him.

Whether encouraged by yourself, your friends, or the Word, don't apologize to anyone for needing a Rest Stop. There are no superheroes in the cemetery. Take time to rest, to recover, to pray, to meditate, to read your Bible, and to regroup.

 *Power Point*
Schedule ONE hour out of your day this week and do....absolutely nothing.

Playing with Pain

I love watching the once and future number one golfer in the world, Tiger Woods. I don't know a thing about golf, but I know a relentless competitor when I see one. Tiger's will to win is unparalleled. Out of his (current) 14 major wins, his 2008 U.S. Open win was phenomenal. To win the tournament in sudden death overtime, with an injured leg! Have you heard of an "ugly win"? Some wins are not pretty—but a win is a win.

The greatness we talked about earlier doesn't just belong to Tiger Woods and Dirk Nowitzkis of this world. It belongs to everyone who makes the decision to keep coming back. We may have to play with pain at times. We may have to attempt victory with one leg.

Your win may not be pretty, easy, or applauded by everyone in your life. But that makes your victories that much sweeter. When you find yourself playing with pain, this is a time to dig deeper, elevate your game, and press in.

Star Stories

Star stories happen after you focus on the blessing and not the bitterness, when God has brought you through situations that have driven others to suicide, though you may be broken, bruised, and battered. As He heals you of your issues, you will, I promise you, be able to look back over your life and be thankful for the peaks *and* the valleys. You will have extracted the purpose from your pain and come through with power. Through the miracle of a touch from God and time, "scar stories" will turn into "star stories."

Like the external scar I told you about in the beginning, I have heart scars too. But now, most of them don't hurt anymore. Now I can share my star stories with others without reliving the pain that produced the scar in the first place.

A Prayer for You

Father, like Your Son's scars, our scars are a testimony. Thank you for the visual and not-so-visual reminders of Your power, love and grace. Help us to deal with the Haters, Waiters and Gaters – the ones we know about and the ones we don't see. Help us to march towards greatness one yard at a time. Most of all, thank You for taking us through our pain and not leaving us in it. In Your Son's Name, Amen.

Reflective Questions

- What little victories can you encourage yourself with?
- How do you neutralize the Haters, Waiters, and Gators in your life?
- Do you have a safe Rest Stop for when you are physically, emotionally, and spiritually exhausted?
- What is your strategy for responding when you hit the Wall?
- What Scar Stories and Star Stories is the world waiting to hear from you?

Finish Well

Chapter 8

I have fought the good fight, I have finished the race, I have kept the faith. 2 Timothy 4:7 (NKJV)

It happens surreptitiously, even stealthily. Our fitness eventually turns to floppiness. What was once high and tight softens and heads south. The buff turns to fluff. For the first time, we're addressed as "ma'am" or "sir." Then, horror of horrors, we start getting called "young lady" and "Pops." We move from daughter and son, to Mom and Dad, Mr. & Ms. (First Name); to Nana and Pop-Pop, to Big Mama and beyond. One day, you are going to phase from getting older to getting old. Sometime later, you are going to die.

Correct that. One day *we* are going to phase from getting older to getting old. *We* are going to die.

The whole point of this book was never about avoiding death, or pretending we're 25 again. (Let's not go *there*.) This whole book is about living well and dying even more so.

As the joke goes, consider the alternative. Getting old or dying young. Hmmm. We are blessed to live in a world where we can choose to live healthy, fit, productive lives even into old age. At the least, we can vastly improve the quality of life we have now, even on a budget.

But, at some time, whether slowly or suddenly, we will not be around. This is not necessarily a bad thing. The way things seem to be going, living forever on this planet is not the most appealing idea.

Two-Minute Warning

There's a country song with the title "Live Like You Were Dying." How appropriate . . . because we are. None of us knows when we will run the final lap, but we do know that the inevitable is coming. It's good to prepare now for the end so we can go about the business of living.

Purpose Point:
Write your own obituary, based on where your life is right now. Now, rewrite it—as if you've realized your Big Dream. How different are the two? What is different about your life's legacy?

I recently attended a luncheon honoring the late renowned Bible teacher Fuschia Pickett, who passed away in 2006. Dr. Myles Munroe, whom she mentored most ably, delivered such a touching homage that I found myself weeping as if I were attending her actual memorial. Five years after your death, what do you think will be said about you? Yes, I know you have absolutely no control over it. But what kind of legacy do you want to leave? Will you leave a legacy of unfulfilled dreams? Of regret and mediocrity? Or one of excellence and destiny? At the end of your life, what seeds that you've planted in your life's garden will bear fruit? Here are some questions you might want to ask yourself as you contemplate your life story.

Are you living your purpose?
Sometimes our purpose changes as we approach our life's end. The professor Randy Paucsh, when diagnosed with terminal pancreatic cancer, spent the last year of his life teaching others his life lesson. He lived his purpose until he took his last breath. A slew of celebrities, including Michael Jackson, died while I was writing this book. A man with a very common name dies—yet I don't have to tell you *which* Michael Jackson I'm talking about. That, people, is impact. His incredible talent, meteoric rise to fame, tumultuous life, and untimely death caused the whole world to give pause on a hot day in late June. More than 30 million people in America alone, and an estimated 1 billion people worldwide, watched his funeral on television. That is mega impact. Whose world are you having an impact on?

Are you fulfilling your passion?

Who is your role model? I propose the Old Testament warrior Caleb. He was still seeking mountains to conquer well into his "retirement years." Age is no determiner of passion. Forget retirement! We have too much to do and too much to offer. Of course, take time to smell the flowers—just don't be planted under them before your time. Not long ago, I met a 91-year-old woman who was running for city council. That lady has *passion*. Recently, I watched someone who could only be described as a mousy middle-aged lady audition on a British talent show known for its acerbic, critical judges. Judge is what they did. They and the audience expected nothing from this plain woman with the sturdy ankles, graying hair, bushy brows, and sagging skin. They got ready to laugh.

But when Susan Boyle opened her mouth, angels flew out. Her voice, so incongruent with her face and body, merged together in beauty and perfection at that one moment in time. The singer became an overnight sensation because of her patience and her *passion*.

When I think of the end of my life, whether it is next week, next month, or in the next few decades, I think of the following.

You're Burning Daylight

What do you want to do?

The saddest words I ever heard my mother say were said while standing at my father's graveside: "We just ran out of time." After 50 years of marriage, they had dreams that never made their way into plans. Many of her dreams died with Daddy.

My father prided himself on autopilot wakeup service at 5 a.m. Anyone who got up a minute later was a slacker. He wanted everyone on his planet to live our lives as if we were burning daylight. Because . . . we are.

What do you want to leave?
In other words, who do you want to bless? The Old Testament patriarch Jacob gave blessing and warning to his sons at the end of his life. This involves practical and spiritual legacies.

I like the idea of seeding into the next generation. I haven't been blessed with children, but some of my young friends at the time of this writing have young children. These kids likely will not remember me when they are grown, but I smile at the thought of being a blessing to them now as much as possible. Someday, they may reflect on their childhood and think, "When I was a kid, I had a purse, a chair, a book that some friend of my mom's gave me. It was my favorite." I want that vaguely remembered older friend to be me.

What do you want to say?
Some things are better left unsaid, the song goes. But some things *need* to be said. What is it that needs to be said? I never liked you? Say I love you to the people you care about in your life. Let old offenses go. Forgiveness is a blessing to the giver and the recipient.

How would you like to leave?

Hold up. I'm not talking about assisted suicide. I'm talking about leaving this stage of life gracefully. We may not be able to choose *when* or *how* we leave, but we can choose *what* we leave. We've all seen sports figures and entertainers stay as long as their legs will carry them to the field or stage; never mind whether they are viable or not. Be the best you can be at this point in the game. Focus is a blessed byproduct of getting older. Your life's purpose is distilled down to its essence. Make sure the distillation is positive.

Second Wind

Begin to move from doing to coaching. Think of yourself as a personal consultant. Look for people who are hungry for what you have to offer. I guarantee they are there. Begin to write down and speak peace and encouragement to everyone you encounter. Plant seeds of love in your giving. My mother used to hand-write greeting cards. Now, she hands out little bookmarks and cards preprinted with Scriptures and inspirational messages. She is sowing love seeds. Speak kind words. Someone wants to hear what you have to say. Someone *needs* what you have to say. Someone needs your life's legacy.

I believe we leave more gracefully when all our affairs are in order. I'm not simply talking about practical things like finances, although that is part of it. I'm talking about saying and doing as much as possible to create an atmosphere of peace wherever you go, both within and without.

The main key to leaving gracefully is leaving without regret. I like to think of the song "My Way." I have not done it all well, or even to your liking, but I have done my best.

How would you like to be remembered? Would you like to be thought of as someone who lived life with passion, purpose, and grace? Or as a bitter, angry person? Will people truly feel a void at your passing, or, like the New Orleans song goes, will they be thinking, "I'm glad you're dead, you rascal you?" Have you lived your life so evilly that people attend your memorial just to make sure you're really dead? (Don't laugh. I've done it a few times.)

I want to be remembered as a woman who lived her life with purpose, with passion, with compassion, and with power. I want the greatness God placed in me to fingerprint the world before I go. I want to leave a lasting legacy of excellence, creativity, and uniqueness that others emulate. I want to be the best *me*—writer, author, speaker, pastor, daughter, sister, friend, and hopefully wife one day—that I can. I want people to be truly blessed by my living and truly saddened by my passing.

 **Purpose Point:**
How would you like to be remembered?

Reflective Questions
- Are your affairs in order? Do you have insurance, a will, a living will, account information and final instructions in writing? Is there anything special, a gift, you'd like to leave for someone?

- Do you have a list of people you'd like contacted?

- Is there anyone you trust to carry out your final wishes?

- Are there any private letters that need to be written and delivered after your death? Are there any special, secret kindnesses you'd like distributed?

- If circumstances permitted, would you want to have a "going-away party," a celebration of your life *before* your death?

- What would you like your final memorial to be? A formal church service, a reception, a party, a simple graveside committal? What location? What music? Flowers and/or charitable contributions? What speakers would you like to have participate?

- What circumstances would need to be in place for you to feel that you've finished well?

It Is Finished

Eight years after I.D. Moore's death, I am still an unapologetic, unashamed, don't-care-if-you-don't-like-it daddy's girl. We were inseparable in my childhood, fought like cats and dogs during my adolescence and young adulthood, and reconciled later with mutual respect.

Let me share a few things about him: The phrase *swagger* was invented for Daddy. His walk rivaled Samuel L. Jackson's and President Barack Obama's. Still sporting a full head of hair in his 70s, he aged well. He wasn't wealthy by any stretch of the imagination. He had a razor-sharp mind, but it was only known by the people who knew, loved, and worked with him. He was devilishly handsome, yet he was devoted to his wife of 50 years— my mother. He wasn't powerful—unless you were lucky enough to live on his planet. He worked his entire career on a most modest salary yet pulled rabbits out of his hat and performed financial miracles that astound me to this day. Daddy, whether asked or unasked, shared admonishments, advice, and arguments with me almost daily. But we also shared an irreversible bond I wish all fathers and daughters could experience. He was gruff, tough, and brusque. Yet, you could wound him with a word. Daddy was . . . incrementally great.

Daddy seeded into my future from my Day One on this planet, and I didn't even realize it. He used to bring home the *Wall Street Journal* for me to read when I was in third grade. He steered me toward the college I attended (a much better choice than my own) and even tried to get me to major in business. Being the creative type, I thought I'd have no use for a business degree. Riiight. He told me, "Charlotte, your future is in religious journalism." Although I'd been writing consistently since I was 14, I couldn't see how that could possibly pan out. Of course, he was right. Again.

The day Daddy went into the hospital for the last time, he was sitting in the emergency room reminding me about a bad business deal I had made two years prior that had left me devastated. It was if he could see into the future that three years later I would encounter nearly the same experience. Amazing. During his final days, I prayed for two things: to let my parents make their 50th wedding anniversary, and to let me be there when he slipped away.

Granted and granted. I was alone at my father's bedside when he took his final breaths. The memory of his last few hours will be with me for the rest of my life. I made a private promise to my father as I stood over his casket for the last time. *The book you are holding is part of the fulfillment of that promise.* Your own life work will be finished someday, but your life legacy can continue forever if you seed into your future.

Thank You for Your Time

My father and I shared an all-too-brief space between hello and goodbye.

At the end of your life, I hope you have spent the space between your hello and your goodbye with gratitude and grace. I hope we all end up saying to God, thank you for giving me *Your* time here on earth. I didn't do everything right, but I did do my best.

I want to thank you for the time you took to read *Preserved for a Purpose*. I hope and pray your time was well spent. I speak God's blessings on you and your Big Dream.

Charlotte Ann Moore

2011